IMMIGRANT 101: How Today's New Americans can Transition Foreign Careers, find Jobs, make Money and cope with life in the United States

By JANET RANGI

This book is dedicated to my late dad for his selfless acts of kindness and humility. To my mom thank you.

Format "IMMIGRATION 101" for print on demand publication with Amazon KDP. Shift content to 6 x 9" cut size. Adjust margins as appropriate and add fold gutter. Add page numbers to the footer and rebuild the table of contents to reflect accurate page numbers. Assure page flow is attractive for reader and assure no orphaned headers at base of pages.

Deliver modified Word docx and pdf file, the latter of which should be loaded as interior file.

Real Reviews, Recommendations and Testimonials from Immigrant Business Directory

Fred: *I do recommend it. It is an eye opener because all information you need to know you'll have it. No questions left unattended to as much as we are many and I call this a big sacrifice since information is power and you hardly find someone sacrificing his or her time to offer all this. Besides that, I am inspired from the videos I've seen hope restored for those ones who lost it. Keep up the good work. God bless you Janet.*

Ella: *Free knowledgeable, inspiring information from one bighearted beautiful lady who sacrifices a lot for others. God bless you Janet.*

Aisha: *I think is the best. It changes people's life. I wish I would be lucky to be one of the chosen one in the DV Lottery. God be there for me and my two kids. Amen*

Rispa: *I can imagine how hard she must work to give us all this information while still trying to balance her life. I just met her today, but I can say this is so impressive. She is very selfless willing to share with everyone about green cards, scholarships, students visa and all that ...keep up Janet. I just love to keep up the good work. You are a true Leader.*

Peris: *Great information from a very selfless lady.*

Edna: *We got the visitor's visa in December 2017. Everyone said it was a miracle to have myself, my husband and three children get the 5-year Visa. What I can say is you have to be confident, show them every reason that will bring you back home and give them a smile! Don't be desperate!*

Nyagwaya: *The information is truthful and reliable. Thanks, Janet, for taking your time to do this, I always wondered where to start from but now I know better.*

Bernard: *If you need the best information for US visas, this is the place to be.*

License Notes

This book is licensed for your personal enjoyment only. This book may not
be re-sold. Thank you for respecting the hard work of this author.

TABLE OF CONTENTS

Introduction

America has long been viewed as the land where dreams can come true. This is according to a survey on immigration conducted by Public Agenda in 2009. America is made up of immigrants and remains the land of opportunity for many around the world. In fact, many people from all over the world dream and desire to move to the United States. Fueled by many desires like adventure, economic, political and religious reasons, this hope has not diminished over the years. This is proved by the fact that immigrants of the past are not different from the immigrants of today. However, studies have shown that recent immigrants also known to some as New Americans are entering the United States with higher education levels compared to previous immigrants. They are all bound by one goal of getting the opportunity to see their dreams fulfilled. America is a representation of every religion and race, and yet, the country is not defined by these things. Rather, the United States is viewed as a beacon of hope and freedom to people all over the world.

My name is Janet Rangi and I was raised in Kenya. I came to the United States in 2003 as a student with 200 dollars in my pocket. I chose to be a VICTOR and not a VICTIM of my circumstances. I am an American citizen by naturalization. I have a Masters' Degree from the University of California Los Angeles (UCLA). I am a Post graduate Student at the University of Texas Rio Grande Valley (UTRGV). I have found a passion in sharing my experiences as a foreign trained immigrant. I blog and vlog with thousands following my content on social media. I have made a life and a career in the United States and I am part of what some would arguably call the American dream. The desire for economic emancipation and career progression was fulfilled and even perhaps exceeded in this journey.

What started as a desire and a dream has become a reality and in the following few chapters I will try and share snippets based on personal experience as a new American. Hopefully you will learn a thing or two on how to make decisions before and after coming to America. Through the course of the book you will read through the lessons I have learnt, mistakes I have made and wisdom that I have gathered over the years. I do this in the hope that perhaps through my journey you will draw your inspiration to dream and fulfil your inspirations and desires. This book will not only serve as an inspiration for one who wants to come to the United States in pursuit of a better life but for anyone who desires to see their dream come true in any part of the world. I am a testament that dreams do come true and that all dreams are valid. In a nut shell, I will cut your learning curve. In my mind I believed there was something bigger than what is my reality. This niggling feeling is what birthed my desire to migrate to the United States, I heard about foreign nurses who were moving to the United States and this desire was born out of wanting a better future. Through my successful transition, I managed to assist others to also immigrate through this process. I have guided them into very lucrative, successful money-making careers and jobs. Through this process I garnered the credibility, the knowledge and experience required to write this book.

In this book I explain the process of making decisions and how I navigated through the various hurdles. Getting here was not an easy process and I feel that I need to help those aspiring to become new Americans to take the same step with a few tips on how to make this dream come true. The process does not begin with getting here but with the purpose of coming and application of the right visa. After getting here there is settling in, adapting to the different culture and systems, and lastly getting the right immigration papers to make the stay permanent. I will give more detailed information about jobs especially in the health care industry and the potential of making lots of money in the millions of dollars over time just by making good decisions. Through this book I will give advice and share through my own personal experiences and the experiences of others who have been through a similar process. I do hope that you enjoy the book as much as I enjoyed writing it.

Transitioning Careers: American education is necessary: Learn more about financing

College expenses range from tuition to housing to bus passes. See how all these costs add up to a college's "sticker price."

In its most recent survey of college pricing, the College Board reports that a moderate college budget for an in-state public college for the 2017–2018 academic year averaged $25,290. A moderate budget at a private college averaged $50,900. But what goes into these costs?

Tuition

Tuition is what colleges charge for the instruction they provide. Colleges charge tuition by the units that make up an academic year, such as a semester or quarter. Tuition at public colleges is often a bargain for state residents, but not for out-of-staters, who often pay double the tuition of residents.

Tuition can vary by major. Students in the sciences, engineering, computing, premed programs, and the fine arts often pay more. For example, at University of Illinois Urbana- Champaign, students enrolled in the College of Engineering pay up to $5,000 more in tuition than students pursuing other majors.

Fees

Colleges charge fees for services. These fees may include the library, campus transportation, student government, and athletic facilities.

Colleges often report a combined tuition and fees figure. According to the College Board, the average cost of tuition and fees for the 2017–2018 school year was $34,740 at private colleges, $9,970 for state residents at public colleges, and $25,620 for out-of-state residents attending public universities.

Housing and Meals

The cost of "room and board" depends on the campus housing and food plans you choose. The College Board reports that the average cost of room and board in 2017– 2018 ranged from $10,800 at four-year public schools to $12,210 at private schools. Colleges also provide room and board estimates for living off campus based on typical student costs.

Books and School Supplies

Most colleges estimate the average costs for required learning materials. Some colleges even include the cost of a computer and computer accessories. The College Board reports the average cost for books and supplies for the 2017–2018 school year was $1,250 at public colleges and $1,220 at private colleges.

Personal and Transportation Expenses

Colleges may estimate some expenses they don't bill you for. These include local transportation, clothing, personal items, entertainment, etc. The College Board reports that expenses in this category for 2017–2018 ran from $2,730 at private colleges to $3,270 at public universities.

Don't Give Up on a College Because of Its Sticker Price

The price of college may seem overwhelming, but college educations come at many different price levels, and financial aid can greatly reduce your cost. The reported college "cost of attendance" is rarely the cost students pay.

Which Colleges Are the Most Expensive?

Colleges with the highest published prices; Columbia University, University of Chicago and Vassar College are among highly selective four-year institutions. These institutions charge more than $56,000 for their sticker price, but many students pay less than this amount to attend.

"Typically, private liberal arts colleges have the highest sticker price, but that doesn't mean they won't be competitive with other universities given their large endowments – especially if you qualify for financial aid and scholarship opportunities," says Amy Goodman, a principal college admissions counselor at IvyWise, a New York-based admissions consulting company.

Some schools with expensive published prices offer generous financial aid packages. In fact, Brown University, Harvard University and Stanford University, to name a few, meet students' full demonstrated need with no loans added to any financial aid package. While these schools charged more than $50,000 in tuition and fees for the 2018-2019 year, they rank highly among U.S. News' Best Value Schools. This ranking takes account the academic quality and the net cost of attendance for a student who received the average level of need-based financial aid.

Which Colleges Are the Least Expensive?

When it comes to published prices, attending a state school as an in-state student might be the least expensive option. Johnson says that's because "everyone who goes to those schools in effect is getting a scholarship – a discount in the cost of education paid by taxpayers."

He says students who choose to go out of state for college forfeit that subsidy. However, there are few states with tuition reciprocity programs. Minnesota, for example, holds an agreement with several neighboring states – Wisconsin, North Dakota, South Dakota, one institution in Iowa and the Canadian province of Manitoba – that reduces nonresident tuition for Minnesotans to attend their public institutions.

Transitioning Careers: Community College vs. University

If you are wondering whether to attend a community college or a university, you should have a solid understanding of the major differences between the two. Keep reading to get the lowdown so you can make an informed decision about the next step in your education.

As a prospective college student, you probably have an idea of what field you want to enter and perhaps which degree you'll need. Beyond that, though, you may be faced with quite a few choices when it comes to your education. One of the biggest decisions you'll make is choosing between a community college and a university.

Community college used to have a reputation of being less academically serious than traditional four-year universities. But a lot has changed in the world of community college. Most importantly, academic standards have risen, as have the qualifications of the teachers.

The choice of community college vs. university really depends on your overall plan for higher education. There are many benefits to beginning your college career at a community college. The quality of education is comparable to traditional institutions of higher education, tuition is more affordable, and the schedule is more flexible.

Some students are still drawn to four-year universities, which offer many things a community college does not, including campus facilities, sports and a more robust student life. But as you'll see, community colleges are changing the landscape of higher education and offering students many more options in pursuing their degree.

Transferring Credits

Most people attend a two-year community college to fulfill their general education requirements and earn an associate's degree. This includes classes that focus on college- level reading and writing, mathematics, science and social science. These general credits can then be transferred to a four-year college to earn a bachelor's degree.

Across the country, community colleges have worked to ensure that their associate's degrees match the general education requirements of most universities, especially local ones. For this reason, it has never been easier for students to transfer credits between the two.

Still, you want to make sure your credits will transfer before you begin your community college studies. Talk to an academic advisor and confirm that you're taking the right classes. You need to have a plan beyond the first two years at community college, otherwise you may wind up repeating several classes once you transfer.

Academic Quality

The primary reason that community colleges have grown so much in popularity is because, by and large, they have significantly improved academic standards over the last 15 to 20 years. An associate's degree from a junior college, as they were more commonly called, used to be looked down upon. It was generally assumed-and usually true that academic standards were lower and the classes not as rigorous.

But these days, it is widely accepted that students learn just as much, sometimes more, attending community college. The curriculum is on par with universities and the classes can be just as challenging. There is still plenty of variety in the industry, but dozens of studies have shown that students transferring from a community college outperform their university counterparts.

One of the main reasons for this level of quality is the faculty. Community colleges now require most professors to have a master's or doctoral degree in their discipline. You may get some younger, less experienced teachers here and there, but there are plenty of seasoned veterans teaching at community colleges.

Many community colleges have reached out to professional industries such as business and science, recruiting career professionals who are actively engaged in their fields and offer unparalleled real-world perspective. Traditional four-year universities typically do not have as much flexibility to do this.

Another big difference is research.

If you take your generals at a major research university, you may be attending lots of crowded classes being taught by graduate students. University professors are often more focused on research than teaching.

But community colleges don't have research grants. The professors are hired to teach, and that is where their focus lies. They can give students more attention and often utilize more effective teaching methods. Because of this, many community college students find that the quality of instruction is better, even if the professor hasn't written esteemed books.

Class Size

Another crucial component to the community college experience is small class size. You won't see many huge, crowded lectures, if any. Most community college classes have twenty students or fewer. This allows for much more interaction and constructive discussion, rather than a one-sided monologue that is common in lower-level university classes.

The small class sizes also contribute to the quality of the teaching, as described above. Professors in small classes are naturally compelled to make the learning process more engaging and interactive. Classroom discussions are more common, and professors are generally more accessible to students. And with fewer papers and exams to grade, professors can give more feedback and develop personal relationships with students.

Compare this with big public research universities. Many of the general education classes have similar curriculum to community colleges. But you will be attending plenty of crowded lectures-some containing more than 150 students-that are often taught by graduate students. Of course, there are exceptions to this, but it is a definite trend in universities. Things get better when you enter your major, but general classes tend to be less intimate and engaging.

Cost of Tuition

Public and private universities are much more expensive, lately the rise in tuition has outpaced average inflation by a wide margin. At a public university, tuition can be upwards of $8,000. It's even higher at private universities. Add on other living expenses and the overall cost, also known as the "sticker price", averages over $20,000.

Across the board, community college is much more affordable. The average tuition is half that of a public university. Part of this is because community colleges are stripped down, avoiding things like big campus infrastructure and extracurricular programs that increase the overhead at large universities.

Books and food still cost as much, but many community college students save money by living at home. Other than this, there won't be a huge difference in your living expenses. But as the cost of tuition keeps rising around the country, more and more people are turning to community college to save money on their first two years of college.

Flexibility

Flexibility is another huge advantage of community colleges, which are typically designed to cater to students who have jobs or families of their own. The fact that students commute to class, rather than live on campus, also makes it necessary to have built-in flexibility.

If you are raising children or work more than a part-time job, then community college is far and away the best option for you. The flexibility of the schedule cannot be found in traditional schools. Community colleges offer many more night classes, and, unlike most universities, class attendance is not a requirement. Your level of participation and what you get out of it are up to you.

Student Culture and Campus Life

This is one area where large universities will always have community colleges beat. Most community colleges don't invest as much in campus facilities, athletic programs, and student clubs/organizations. That makes it more affordable, but many students feel the need to have "the college experience", which includes living in student dorms and participating in campus life.

You won't find nearly as much of this culture at community colleges, and certainly no fraternities or sororities. But you may be surprised by some of the campuses in the nation's larger community colleges. Many have invested substantially in campus facilities like student centers, campus dining, computer labs and state-of-the-art classrooms.

Some community college students who transfer to big universities have an adjustment period. It is easy to feel alienated when you're new to an environment and most other people have already been there for two years. Most universities provide services for transfer students that make it easier to engage in the social life of the campus.

If you'd like to play sports but don't feel that you're ready for NCAA Division I competition, you may be able get more playing time and better enjoy the sport at a community college. Many of the larger schools have active and diverse athletics programs, including competitive football, basketball, track and field, baseball, volleyball and more.

Transitioning careers: How to obtain financial aid in United States

Student financial aid in the United States is funding that is available exclusively to students attending a post-secondary educational institution in the United States. This funding is to assist in covering the many costs incurred in the pursuit of post-secondary education. Financial aid is available from federal, state, educational institutions, and private agencies (foundations), and can be awarded in the forms of grants, education loans, work-study and scholarships. In order to apply for federal financial aid, students must first complete the Free Application for Federal Student Aid (FAFSA).

International Scholarships

There are many resources available to students to search for scholarships, and there are also many services that charge students for either access to their scholarship database or to conduct a scholarship search on a student's behalf. If you have the time and available resources, most of the scholarship searches can be found online for free. InternationalScholarships.com is one that offers a free scholarship search, and with a little research you can find many more out there. Take your time, do your homework and you will be able to find all the information you need.

For international students hoping to study in the US, scholarships can be an invaluable help toward financing your goals. Whether you are an incoming first year, a student going on to graduate school, or simply returning to college for a new year, there is financial assistance out there for you.

Ask Your School

No matter where you live or attend school, your first step when searching for scholarships should be your school's financial aid office. Most colleges offer scholarship programs specifically for international students attending the institution. Check out your school's financial aid website or call or email the office if you can't find what you're looking for.

Am I eligible for a scholarship?

Eligibility for a scholarship depends entirely on the scholarship; there is no general rule of thumb on whether you are eligible for a financial award. Some scholarships require students to have a certain TOEFL score; some ask that you are from a certain country; some ask for you to have a certain grade point average. You will need to do your own research to see if you are eligible for a scholarship. It can be confusing but remember that college admissions officers and financial aid experts are there to help you find as much money as you qualify for.

How do I apply?

As with eligibility, there is no set rule on how to apply for scholarships. While some just require you to complete an application form, others may require a specially written piece of work, or for you to be pursuing studies in a certain field. If you find a scholarship for which you think that you may be eligible, contact the award administrator of that award. All the scholarships found in the InternationalStudent.com Scholarship search contain contact details of the award administrator.

Student Loans for Immigrants

You should always carefully evaluate how much money you will need to study in the USA. Then you will need to research and apply for scholarships, financial aid from your school, and find money from any other source, including family funds. After exhausting these avenues, most international students still have a funding gap, and that's where international student loans come in.

Federal student loans are popular with US students studying in the US, but they are not available to international students. Instead, international students are eligible for international student loans, specialized private education loans available to international students studying in the US.

International Student Loans are now a very realistic way to finance your education in the US. Loans are very flexible and can offer loan amounts high enough to pay for your entire education, but with extended repayment terms and reasonable interest rates, so you can afford the repayment after you graduate.

Cosigners

Most international students applying for loans must have a US cosigner in order to apply. A cosigner is legally obligated to repay the loan if the borrower fails to pay. The cosigner must be a permanent US resident with good credit who has lived in the US for the past two years. The cosigner is often a close friend or relative who can assist in getting credit, since most international students cannot receive credit on their own. If you're not able to find a cosigner see if there are no cosigner loans available to you.

Interest

Interest is the amount charged by the lender in addition to the amount of money that you borrowed. The interest rate is calculated based on an index plus a margin that will add an additional percentage interest rate depending on your co-signer's creditworthiness. The two most common indexes used for international students are the Prime Rate and LIBOR Rate.

• Prime Interest Rate – This index is determined by the federal funds rate which is set by the US Federal Reserve.

• LIBOR – The LIBOR (London Interbank Offered Rate) is based on the British Bankers' Association and is used on the London interbank market. The rate is an average of the world's most creditworthy bank's interbank deposit rates for overnight and one-year terms.

When evaluating the loan, the lender will clarify which index the plan uses. Then, there will be an additional margin that will be added based on the borrower's individual criteria, including the co-signer's credit history. Based on their creditworthiness, an additional interest rate will be added to the index. This will be the total interest you owe. When your application is approved, your specific margin will be disclosed to you, at which point you can accept or refuse the loan.

Repayment

Repayment will vary depending on the loan option you choose. Since most international students are not able to work while they study in the US, repayment must be considered as an extremely important feature in your loan. You will need to consider how much the monthly payments will be, when payments will begin, and how long you will be able to defer paying back the loan. The repayment period generally ranges from 10-25 years, but the larger the loan, the longer the repayment period. The standard repayment plan options are:

• Full Deferral: Students can defer payment until 6 months after graduation as long as full-time status is maintained. Students can defer payments for a maximum of four years, which is the typical length of a degree.

• Interest Only: International students only pay the interest while in school, up to four consecutive years, and can defer the principal until 45 days after graduation, or when the student drops their course load to part-time.

• Immediate Repayment: Payments on both interest and principal are due immediately once the loan has been dispersed.

How Can I Get a Loan Without a Cosigner?

You may be discouraged at how difficult it can be for an international student to find someone to cosign their private loan. Don't be discouraged but focus on those careers that you will easily find employment immediately after graduation. For instance, focus on STEM (Science Technology, Engineering and Mathematics). Quite honestly focus on courses in the medical field such as Nursing, Dentistry, Medicine, Pharmacy and Physical Therapy. These jobs not only make it easier for you to get legal working status in the United States, but they will enable online lenders to trust that your repayment abilities without a co-signer. Stay tuned because in the coming chapters I will give more detailed information about jobs in medical fields and the potential of making lots of money in the millions of dollars over time by making good decisions early and following your passions. The online lenders below have not been verified by me personally but seem credible. This is good to know information to give you hope and a variety of options.

According to Stilt, there are several online lenders designed specifically for international students and others who may have trouble qualifying for a loan or getting a cosigner. Stilt is specifically designed for international students and others who may have difficulty obtaining a private or federal loan in the US. Stilt lends to immigrants, including international students and DACA holders, who can't get a cosigner and have competitive interest rates starting at 7.99%. Stilt is the top pick, as they have the fewest qualification requirements. The loan process is quick — you can get a decision within 24 hours after a complete application. The funds can be in your account in as quickly as 1 business day after the promissory note is signed. Stilt doesn't partner with universities, so you are eligible to apply irrespective of the university you attend. Stilt is also the only option if you want to refinance your international student loan without a cosigner. You can also start building credit with a Stilt loan.

Like Stilt, MPOWER also focuses on international students and has a minimum 7.99% interest rate. To make up for the lack of cosigner, however, MPOWER tends to give loans to students they feel have high earnings potential. Mpower partners with universities and provides loans only for a few majors. To be eligible for Mpower, you should be attending a school supported by Mpower and be in the last 2 years of your education. The loans have up to 10 years repayment period. Because of this, it can be difficult for undergraduate students and students at lower-tier universities to qualify. On average, it takes 3 weeks for an end-to-end process with Mpower, and the funds are disbursed directly to the school.

Another international student loan company is Prodigy Finance. They have seen great success and hope to grow tremendously in the future. The downside, though, is that they have tough qualification guidelines. The list of partner universities and majors are limited. Prodigy is focused on loans to international students who attend MBA programs. They only offer loans to students at the highest ranked universities and even restrict the areas of study that they will cover. The loans are originated from a U.K.-based entity, and the repayments are not reported to credit bureaus in the U.S.

Jobs for immigrants: How to Work in the U.S. with a Student Visa

During your time as an international student in the U.S., you may decide you want to get a job—whether it's to lighten the load of your tuition, gain some work experience, or just have a little extra pocket money to spend.

Keep in mind, though, that as an international student who is in the U.S. on a visa, you can't just go out and get any job you want. There are regulations you must follow. Working illegally will land you in hot water with the U.S. government. And nobody wants that.

What to Do First

Before you begin the process of finding a job, contact your Designated School Official (DSO). That's the person your school designated to assist international students. If you are already a student, you likely already made contact with your DSO when you arrived. But if you haven't, any school official should be able to point you to the right person or department.

Your DSO will help you apply for a Social Security Number (required for all students working in the U.S.) and guide you through the appropriate steps.

Employment Opportunities

The Department of Homeland Security outlines four ways for international students to legally work in the U.S. on an F1 (student) visa:

• On-Campus Employment

• Off-Campus Employment

• Curricular Practical Training (CPT)

• Optional Practical Training (OPT)

On-Campus Employment

On-campus employment is the most freely available to F1 students and refers to work that takes place on campus or at an "educationally affiliated off-campus location."

According to the Department of Homeland Security, being "educationally affiliated" means the off-campus location must meet at least one of these two criteria:

• Associated with the school's established curriculum

• Related to contractually-funded research projects at the post-graduate level

• The latter part of that definition is worth emphasizing, as many colleges and universities have buildings and educational partnerships all over town.

So, in other words, you could work somewhere on your school's campus, such as a bookstore, library, dorm, or cafeteria. Or you could work somewhere like an off-campus research lab that is affiliated with your school.

This is the only type of employment you can pursue starting in your first academic year, and you may apply as early as 30 days before classes start.

Work hours are limited to 20 hours per week while school is in session, but you can work full time during holidays and vacation periods. If you choose to work more than one on- campus job, your total combined hours per week cannot exceed 20 hours.

Off-Campus Employment

Jobs outside of your school are only available to international students who have completed one full academic year and who have a qualifying economic hardship or an emergent circumstance.

According to the DHS, a qualifying economic hardship entails "new, unexpected circumstances beyond [your] control," such as:

• Loss of financial aid or on-campus employment (if the student is not at fault)

• Large increases in tuition or living costs

• Substantial decrease in the relative value of currency the student depends upon to pay expenses

• Unexpected changes in the financial conditions for a student's sources of financial support

• Unexpectedly large medical bills not covered by insurance

• Other substantial, unexpected expenses

Emergent circumstances are defined as "world events that affect a specific group of F-1 students and which causes them to suffer severe economic hardship, including, but not limited to natural disasters, wars and military conflicts, national or international financial crises."

Certain regulatory requirements may be suspended for students that are from parts of the world that are experiencing emergent circumstances. This is known as Special Student Relief.

To apply for off-campus employment, contact your Designated School Official (DSO). He or she must approve the reason and recommend off-campus employment as the first part of the application process.

Note that you cannot begin working while your application is still being processed by the

Immigration and Customs Enforcement. Apply early so you'll be ready to go when you receive an offer of employment. If approved, you may work 20 hours per week.

Curricular Practical Training (CPT)

Curricular Practical Training (CPT) should be part of your school curriculum. It is designed to give you real-world experience in your field of study, like an internship or practicum with a partnering employer, the DHS explains.

Unlike other employment categories, CPT can be full time, with no weekly hour limit. You can also have more than one CPT authorization at the same time.

Keep in mind that if you participate in a year or more of full-time CPT, you are ineligible for Optional Practical Training, or OPT (which you can read more about below).

To qualify for CPT, you must have completed one full academic year, unless you're a graduate student whose program requires immediate CPT. In any case, the DHS advises seeking your DSO as your first step.

Optional Practical Training (OPT)

Optional Practical Training (OPT) refers to temporary employment relating to your field of study (working at a TV station, for example, would qualify if you're studying journalism). Eligible students can receive up to 12 months of OPT employment.

There are two types of OPT:

• Pre-completion OPT: This option is available once you have completed one full academic year at a U.S. college or university. You can work up to 20 hours a week when school is in session or full time when it is not.

• Post-completion OPT: You can apply for this option after completing your studies. Those who are authorized for post-completion OPT can work either part time or full time.

You'll need approval from your DSO, who will then endorse your application and help you submit it to U.S. Citizenship and Immigration Services.

Keep in mind that if you participate in both pre-completion and post-completion OPT, the 12-month maximum work period is divided between the two. If you participated in 9 months of pre-completion OPT during your time as a student, you can only participate in 3 months of post-completion OPT after you graduate.

STEM OPT Extension

If you finish your studies and participate in a period of post-completion OPT, you might then qualify for the STEM OPT extension, which is a 24-month period of temporary training that directly relates to your program of study.

This extension is only available if your employer is enrolled in the E-Verify program and if you have a degree in one of the STEM (science, technology, engineering, or mathematics) fields on this list.

Confused about the difference between Curricular and Optional Practical Training? Check out this helpful cheat sheet!

Coping with life in the United States: Don't Try to Get Around the Rules

If you're considering running your own side gig (like this student who turned his dorm room into a restaurant), know that the U.S. government views that as a job.

To make it legal, you'd have to qualify and apply for OPT, which we covered above.

As you take the next steps toward employment, be mindful that working without adequate authorization can lead to deportation and your inability to return to the United States.

Don't risk it. It's not worth jeopardizing all the effort and expenses you've invested this far. Use the resources available to you, starting with your own school.

Coping with life in the United States: Apply for the work visa early

H1B VISA

The H1B visa is a temporary or non-immigrant "specialty occupation" US visa, which means the holder is employed in a position that requires specialized skills or knowledge.

Jobs that suit the H1B visa typically need a university degree or equivalent (which can mean 3 years' work experience for each year that would normally be spent at university). The position should be one that would normally require that level of experience.

The visa is valid for three years, with one possible additional three-year extension, making six years' maximum stay in total.

Any application must be sponsored by a valid company. So, the individual must have an offer of work, education, or internship prior to submitting the application.

The H1B Cap

USCIS normally issue a maximum of 65,000 regular H1B visas each year, with some exceptions:

The first 20,000 visas awarded to people who hold master's degrees or higher do not count against the limit.

Visas for people entering the US to work in higher education or in affiliated research/non- profit organizations may also be exempt from the cap.

6800 visas are normally reserved for citizens of Chile and Singapore, under the special H1-B1 visa. This number is deducted from the total (65,000 regular plus 20,000 masters') visa allocation.

Because of the strict limits, visas are granted on a lottery basis. This means there is no guarantee that, even if you qualify, you will be awarded your visa. (Of course, if you do not apply, you cannot win the lottery.)

How to Get H1B Visa

Because of the limited number of visas issued, there is a specific window for applications, which usually starts on April 1st for the fiscal year starting October 1st of the following year. So, you can apply from April 1st, 2019 for entry in the year starting October 1st, 2020.

Transferring a H-1B Visa to a Green Card

The process of getting a Green Card through employment is called the H-1B to Green Card transfer.

The H1B visa is the most popular non-immigrant work visa for the U.S. It signifies that the holder of the visa has an occupation which is desirable in the country and has completed extensive education and training. H1B visas are given to people for a maximum of 6 years. After the 6 years, they are required to return to their home country. The U.S grants a grace period of 10 days after the H1B visa expires for employees to make arrangements for their return or extend their stay.

What is the H1B to Green Card Process?

A lot of H1B visa holders want to become permanent residents of the United States. This can be done by getting an American Green Card. Since the H1B visa is of dual intent, this means that those who have it are eligible to apply for permanent residence.

The process of getting a U.S green card from the H1B visa is called the H1B to Green Card transfer or the Employment Based Green Card. Besides this, there are also other types of Green Cards such as:

- Family Based Green Card

- Political Asylum Based Green Card

- Adoption Based Green Card

- Refugee Based Green Card

- Diversity Based Green Card

For the Employment Based Green Card, it can take months or years to get the Green Card. Several steps are required, and agencies require extensive documentation. The procedure can become complicated, so most agencies recommend hiring an experienced attorney. They can guide you through the documentation and deadlines for a smoother transition.

Here are the steps of transferring from H1B to Green Card:

- Getting PERM Labor Certification.

- Filing Form I-140, Immigrant Petition for Alien Worker.

- Filing Form I-485, Adjustment of Status.

- Each one has its own procedures and documents you need to submit, so the article will go through how you can successfully complete each one. The most important factor you need to know is that the Employment Based Green Card process must be initiated by your employer in the United States. The employee or anyone else cannot start the process of applying for the Green Card.

Due to this, before you start your process to get a Green Card, you need to find a U.S employer willing to hire and sponsor you.

Coping with life in the United States: Housing and Accommodation

In the USA, it is more common for people to buy their own home than to rent. No matter which of those options you choose, a realtor may help you throughout the process. Finally, no matter if you move to New York or San Francisco, don't forget to set up your utilities in your new home.

There are several destinations in the United States which are, and always have been, popular among immigrants and expats. New York is probably the most famous of them, but San Francisco, Miami, and Chicago also make it to the top ranks. At the same time, however, there are many downsides to living in these cities, such as the population density and the high rents. It thus makes sense to take a second look at the cities Americans are migrating to and the areas which have a promising economic upswing ahead of them. Smaller cities are always a better option if you want to avoid competition and make more money in your field of study.

Buying vs. Renting

Buying a house or an apartment in the USA is a straight-forward procedure. In general, there are many properties for sale and realtors focus largely on bringing sellers and buyers together. However, this doesn't mean that you do not have to jump some bureaucratic hurdles. As most expats do not have much of a credit history in the United States, getting a mortgage is probably the most difficult part. Those who come to the country for a short time only are usually better off renting a home. In some cities, it may be easy to find an affordable house or apartment. In others, you may need strong nerves and a big budget to find a place to live. In any case, you should take a second look at the rental agreement and make sure you understand it before signing it.

Housing and Utilities

One of the places that you will see a lot of variation in the United States is in housing and living accommodations. The average apartment in the United States can run anywhere from $500 (one bed room apartments in more rural areas) to $1,500 (3-bedroom apartment in urban areas).

This price could also vary depending on which utilities are included in your rent. Many renters in college towns will include a few utilities in the monthly rent, but that is not always the case. Consult your contract to determine what is included in your rent. Here are some of the most common values you will see for different utilities:

• Electric: $50 to $100 per month, depending on the size of your apartment and if there are energy efficient appliances and lights used. If your heating is electric, it can make your costs up to $150 per month.

• Gas: Not in all apartments. If used for cooking, it will only run from $10 to $15 a month, depending on how much you cook. If used for heating, it can run upwards of $50-$100/month.

• Internet: Averages $45-$50 per month.

• Cellular service: Most services average $50 a month, unless you include a data plan, which can push it to upwards of $100 per month.

• Water, sewer, and trash. Many times, this is included in the rent because your landlord will cover it for the entire apartment building. If you do have to pay, however, most municipalities will bill you every quarter (3 months) and it will cost approximately $50-$75 every quarter, depending on the region you reside in.

When you are living in the United States, you will likely want to budget approximately $1000 – $1500 per month for housing and utilities.

Other Costs

Here are some other costs that may come up during your time in the United States. These numbers are just to help you determine how much you may spend

• Groceries for one person, for one week, can run between $20 and $40, depending on what you diet consists of. A gallon of milk costs approximately $3.50, a loaf of bread is about $2.50, Rice is about $1 per pound, and eggs are about $2.00 per dozen. Fresh produce costs quite a bit and will fluctuate depending on which fruits and vegetables are in season.

• Gas costs approximately $3.50 per gallon. If you are lucky enough to be in an area that has public transportation, you can get a monthly pass for approximately $50-$60 (some areas have discounts for students).

• Clothes are relatively expensive unless you go to a large chain department store (Wal-Mart, etc). A pair of jeans can cost you around $40.

If you are looking for more information about the cost of living in the United States, look at the Number prices for various items; these numbers are based on user input from those who live and/or visit the United States. You can also look at Find the Data, which also does the same sort of user-based input values. The United States Census Bureau puts out relevant information about the cost of living in various areas of the United States.

Coping with life in the United States: Transportation

Cost of transportation in USA

It would be easy to assume that public transportation is cheaper, because a bus token is far less expensive than gas, but those are not the only costs to consider. Taking public transportation takes a lot of extra time. You will have to get to the station, possibly in your car where you will have to pay for parking, then get on one or several trains and buses to get to your actual destination. It can easily turn what would have been a 20-minute commute into an hour long one. When it comes to the actual money you would spend on using your car over public transport, the public transport is likely going to be cheaper. Passes for the public transportation are somewhere between $20 and $50 a week, depending on where you live. If you must park your car at the station you can add on another $50 a week at $10 per day. That means that your personal finance would be impacted at about $100 a week, in the city if you drive your car to the station. It drops to less than $50 if you can catch a bus close to home.

If you drive your car you have a lot of costs to consider. Even if the car is paid off you are still paying insurance at a rate of $100 a month, if you have a relatively cheap policy. That adds $25 a week. You can also figure a tank of gas a week at an average cost of $2.50/gallon for a 10-gallon tank. That adds another $25 per week.

Coping with life in the United States: Learn more about credit

The importance of good credit

The importance of good credit can't be underestimated — maintaining a healthy credit score allows you to focus on wealth-building and setting yourself up for success in the future. General advice is to apply for a credit card early, use that credit card to pay bills and essential items. At the end of each month pay off the credit card using cash money from your debit card. After six months you will be able to create a credit profile in the United States and lenders will begin to trust you. Continue this process during your entire stay in the United states. Borrow what you can afford. Many banks provide both credit and debit cards including American Express which is my personal favorite. Most places accept Visa and Master Cards.

You can pay off debt faster

Whether you're hoping to take out an auto loan for a new car or refinance credit card debt into a personal loan, the higher your credit score, the lower your interest rate will be. This means that you'll be able to pay off your loans faster because you'll be paying less interest and more of your payment will go towards the principal balance.

The higher your credit score rating, the less interest you'll have to pay. You can get out of debt many months or even years faster than you previously thought.

You can afford better housing

When it comes to the importance of good credit, you could see a big payoff in your home. As a renter, your landlord may use your credit score as a determining factor of your personal characteristics.

Your credit score is an indicator of whether you pay rent on time and if you'll be a good tenant. The higher your credit score, the more likely you'll be able to qualify for your ideal apartment. You could also have additional leverage when it comes to negotiating rental terms based on your good history of credit.

If you're in the market to purchase a home, a bank or mortgage company will be looking very closely at your finances. Your credit score is used to determine how big of a home loan you'll be eligible for.

An excellent credit score means qualifying for a lower interest rate on your mortgage, which could mean significant savings over a 30-year term loan, and ultimately being able to afford a bigger and better home.

You can land a better-paying job

Depending on your chosen career field, your credit score could greatly affect your ability to get the job you want. Much like a landlord, some employers view your credit score as evidence of your ability to be responsible, show up to work on time, and be a contributing member of the team.

Up to 47 percent of employers run credit checks on their employees. A poor credit rating could mean less pay, and possibly having to settle for a different position or job altogether.

Your monthly bills will be lower

You may not realize it, but your creditworthiness plays a large part in your monthly household bills. For example, many car insurance companies view your credit history as a direct correlation to the likelihood of whether you'll be in an accident, as well as your ability to make your insurance payments on time.

Utility companies also routinely check credit scores before turning on electricity, water, and gas services to a place of residence. Having a low credit rating could mean that you're required to pay a deposit upfront before being able to use their services.

You can have a better retirement

Establishing a better credit score throughout your adult life will allow you to pay off debt and have more financial freedom. This ultimately enables you to start saving more money towards other goals.

Instead of forking over a lot of money towards interest payments, you'll be able to prioritize financial goals beyond just paying debt, like having a good quality of life during retirement. What's more, many people reduce costs by downsizing their cars or homes as they enter retirement. Having a strong savings fund will lessen the number of lifestyle changes you make when you stop working.

Don't underestimate the importance of good credit. Proper credit management and smart spending habits will help you.

Coping with life in the United States: How to Handle Authorities

What to Do If the Police Stop You

Being stopped by a police officer is scary. As citizens and members of the public it is our responsibility to know the law and our hope that cops will be officers of justice. But citizen rights are not always respected. So, in an interaction with an officer it's important to avoid doing anything that could result in a risk to our safety. This instructable will walk you through everything you need to know to be safe while interacting with the police.

All the information in this guide is straight from the American Civil Liberties Union.

General Guidance for Dealing with the Police

• What you say to the police is always important. What you say can be used against you, and it can give the police an excuse to arrest you, especially if you badmouth a police officer.

• You must show your driver's license and registration when stopped in a car. Otherwise, you don't have to answer any questions if you are detained or arrested, with one important exception. The police may ask for your name if you have been properly detained, and you can be arrested in some states for refusing to give it. If you reasonably fear that your name is incriminating, you can claim the right to remain silent, which may be a defense in case you are arrested anyway.

• You do not have to consent to any search of yourself, your car or your house. If you DO consent to a search, it can affect your rights later in court. If the police say they have a search warrant, ASK TO SEE IT.

• Do not interfere with, or obstruct the police, as you can be arrested for it.

35

Remember:

• Think carefully about your words, movement, body language, and emotions.

• Do not get into an argument with the police.

• Anything you say or do can be used against you.

• Keep your hands where the police can see them.

• Do not run. Do not touch any police officer.

• Do not resist even if you believe you are innocent.

• Do not complain on the scene or tell the police they are wrong or that you are going to file a complaint.

• Do not make any statements regarding the incident.

• Ask for a lawyer immediately upon your arrest.

• Remember officer badge & patrol car numbers.

• Write down everything you remember ASAP.

• Try to find witnesses & their names & phone numbers.

• If you are injured, take photographs of the injuries as soon as possible, but make sure you seek medical attention first.

• If you feel your rights have been violated, file a written complaint with police department internal affairs division or civilian complaint board

Transitioning as Foreign Nurse Professional in America

America has the largest healthcare budget per person in the world and one of the reasons for such a large healthcare budget is the need for specialized labor. Specialized healthcare professionals are expensive to train and take a long time to train. This has created a great need of healthcare professionals with the American educational system being incapable churning out enough professionals to be able to work in the sector. Even if the professionals were trained in the United States the high cost the specialized training required would make the cost of healthcare delivery even more expensive to the American citizen.

To plug the gap the health authorities have resorted to encouraging foreign healthcare professionals to come to America for work to help bridge the gap that is currently being felt in the healthcare industry. Healthcare professionals from middle income and third world nations have thus been moving in droves and migrating to the United States where they are guaranteed of good working conditions and excellent salaries. This has made the United States the largest employer of migrant healthcare workers in the world.

Foreign Educated Health Professionals possess skills that are valuable in America. But it is necessary for a foreign educated nurse to meet the necessary basic training and regulatory requirements to secure an employment opportunity in the health care sector. It is through the following process that I transitioned my foreign nursing credentials.

Transitioning to the American Nursing Workforce requires a detailed process in licensure for foreign educated nurses. This write up will show the necessary steps required for a foreign healthcare professional to transition into the American healthcare sector. The requirements to transition are outlined below.

Attain the educational requirements

To transition smoothly you will be required to attain educational programs and licenses from your country of origin. This will qualify you to advance your career as a nurse in the American health care setup.

As a foreign Nurse seeking opportunities to live and work in America permanently. You must have;

• Undertaken and graduated from a certified Registered Nursing Program

• Registered and licensed as a Nurse (Registered Nurse)

• At least Two (2) years of clinical practice as a Registered Nurse

Majority of the American States have the mandatory completion of the Foreign Educated Nurses (FEN) course. This is refresher course will ensure the foreign nurse gets licensed. The course entails 120 hours clinical practice and 120 hours in the classroom under the direct overseeing or supervision by a registered nurse

Language Proficiency Test

Based on the country of origin, it is highly likely that you will be required to undertake one of the describe tests as outlined below:

• Test of English for International Communication (TOEIC), English as a Foreign Language (TOEFL) or the International English Language Testing System (IELTS).

Recruitment agencies prefer that International clients take either TOEFL or (IELTS).

• The test administration will need to send result of the Foreign Nurse to the state board that they are applying to.

The National Council Licensing Examination – Registered Nurse (NCLEX – RN)

The Foreign Educated Nurse Professional must enroll with the Pearson VUE (Virtual University Enterprises) on a scheduled day and site to take the (NCLEX – RN). You have to exam pass this exam to secure Licensure in the United States. Unlike previously, the NCLEX examination is now offered in multiple countries outside the United States which is good for nurses looking to work in the United states. Personally, I came as a student and therefore I was able to take the NCLEX in the United States.

Seeking an American Based employer or a Recruiting agency

In America nursing recruiters assist Foreign Educated Nurse Professionals in securing a position as a registered nurse. Nursing recruiters act also act as or serve as US based employers. Their main role is to assist the Registered Nurse in attaining an immigration Visa. This is inclusive of searching for a job with one of the Health facilities or Hospitals that they collaborate with. I have heard about friends who came through agents such as Avant and Adevia Interstaff Health Care professionals. These are just two examples but there are many other online agents and immigration lawyers who can assist you to navigate the process of coming to the United States as a nurse.

Registered Nurse Immigrant Green Card Visa

To secure an immigrant visa as a Registered Nurse the following documents are required:

• Supporting evidence is required that you as a Foreign Educated Nurse Professional has United States based employer acting as your petitioner for your immigrant visa. Nursing recruiters can be your petitioner.

• The Visa Screen Certificate (VSC). This document is given by the International Commission of Health Care (ICHP), a division or agency of the Commission on Graduates of Foreign Nursing Schools (CGFNS).

Visa Interview and Medical Examination

Note that timeline of processing the visa will be based on factors that based on your personal factors such as how fast you respond when documents are required from you. After a successful approval of visa immigration petition

• Your file is sent to the National Visa Center (NVC)for processing by the United States Citizenship and Immigration Service

• NVC forwards the file to the closest US embassy where the visa is issued

• A letter will be sent by the NVC indicating the scheduled date for the visa interview which you will also need to carry with you for official purposes during the interview

• Next will be the medial exam. The letter from the NVC will outline a list of designated physicians that you will contact for the medical process

Registered Nurse Job Offer and Employment Medical Exam

The RN agency/recruiter or employer will have secured a job placement with one of their partner hospitals prior to the visa interview. At this point please provide the RN specialty checklist as well as your résumé. A second medical examination will be required which will be given to the employing hospital. Requirements of the exam vary from hospital to hospital.

Registered Nurse Resuscitation Certification

The following resuscitation certification is required; however, they will dependent on area of practice and guidelines of the hospital.

• Basic Life Support (BLS) certification

• Pediatric Advanced Life Support (PALS) certification

• Advanced Cardiac Life Support (ACLS) certification

You can acquire this certification upon arrival in America. Be certain that the provider of these courses is accredited by the American Heart Association.

Transitioning as a Foreign Trained Dentist in America

After the success of my transition to the United States, I helped others to come to the United States as foreign trained dentists. The process involved passing examinations and going back to University in the United states before they practice dentistry. This was a very insightful experience and formed the basis I have used to mentor others through the system of getting jobs and migrating to the United States. These are some of the procedures the foreign dentist I know personally followed in to start working in the United States. Most of the information is online but through this book you get firsthand information from those who have lived the process. Keep in mind to apply as many schools as possible. Fees are expensive but if you can demonstrate that you have a close family member or friend willing to co-sign on your loans that will greatly help. Also go through the Chapter where I wrote about financial aid and getting loans without a cosigner. If you have a green card obviously it's much easier because you will get financial aid for the entire program. If you are denied admission the first time do not quit, this is normal. Make your application stronger by attaining some clinical experiences in the United States especially in health care or work as a dental assistant. Humble yourself and do not feel less by doing things you consider below your education standards. Believe me your personal statement showing your willingness to help people could be the major determining factor whether you get admission or not. Remember the programs are competitive with most students coming from the Asian Continent. If you are an immigrant from other continents aside from Asia, you will probably bring some newer perspective and diversity to the foreign Dental school programs in the United States.

Foreign educated dentists have an opportunity to practice in the United States, they can do so by attending an American Dental Program in the United states. This is earned by completing an Advanced Standing Program (ASP). To qualify for the ASP, you to be initially trained through the traditional accredited dental curriculum from your country of origin. As part of their application process, various ASP's will require you to do case presentations, a psychomotor bench test or case presentations.

Entry requirements for the Advanced Standing Program

• Passing the National Board Dental Examination (NBDE) Part 1 and 2

• Taking the Test of English as a Foreign Language (TOFEL)

• Graduation from a 4-year Dentist Program from your country

• Transcripts from Dental School

• Evaluation of All transcripts

National Board Dental Examination has the objective of assisting the state boards in evaluating the qualifications of US and internationally Educated Dentists who desire to acquire licensure and to practice as dentists. Students must therefore attain a passing grade in courses covered by the Boards of examinations. In-order for you to be admitted to the US dental schools as Foreign Educated Dentist, transcripts will be evaluated by respective organizations. Just to give you real world examples, the two dentists I know attended University of the Pacific Arthur A. Dugoni School of Dentistry in San Francisco and Loma Linda University in San Bernardino. Both these Schools are found in the state of California but there several other program you will find online. Upon graduation and licensure, you can live and work anywhere in the United States. Many dental employers will sponsor your work permit through H1B visa and at which time you may qualify for green card or permanent residency. From experience, Dentist can earn 150- 350 thousand dollars per year, but these figures could be larger if they open private practice. Use this as a guide to calculate your financial responsibilities. These are the commonly used credential evaluation services but remember to follow guidelines from your specific University of interest that offers degrees to foreign trained dentist.

• World Education Services Inc

The Credential Advantage Package (ICAP) - Fees $205

WES Basic Evaluation - Fees $160

Timeline Seven Business Days after Receipt

Refer to this link for more information https://www.wes.org/evaluations-and-fees/professional-license-certification/dentistry-dentaltech/

• Educational Credentials Evaluators Inc

Course by Course evaluation - $160

High school &University Level course by course evaluation - $ 195

Timeline Seven Business Days after Receipt

Refer to this link for more information
https://www.ece.org/ECE/Individuals/Services--Fees

• Language Proficiency Test

Based on the country of origin, it is highly likely that you will be required to undertake the English as a Foreign Language exam (TOEFL)

https://www.ets.org/toefl offers resource indicating testing centers and the dates

https://www.ielts.org/ offers English exams centers, exam fees are $242.

Under these sites navigate to create an account and choose your country and you will get to see where and when the exams will be offered. Take note of the fees you need to pay.

2nd Option - Faculty D.D.S./D.M.D.

Besides the Advanced Standing Programs, American Dental schools have a second option for foreign dental students. This alternative is known as the faculty Doctor of Dental Surgery/ Doctor of Medicine in Dentistry (D.D.S./D.M.D.) option for foreign students who are full time faculty members. This option is usually discussed during the job interview and at this point it is when you will get to know if the school offers this alternative.

Currently no schools are offering this alternative. Note that this program is customized to meet the needs of the individual seeking to pursue this option.

Resource reference - American Student Dental Association (ASDA) https://www.asdanet.org/index/dental-student-resources/tips-for-international-dental-students offers a guide on the enroll process in American Dental Schools for Internationally Trained Dentists

3rd Option - Residency Program

Depending on the type of Degree, Residency programs are between 2 – 6 years. This option allows majority foreign educated students to transition, therefore this program is usually completed in concurrence of earning a masters or doctorate degree. The National Matching Services assist in the matching of the six categories of residency programs in the selection of students this can be found on their website https://natmatch.com/dentres/aboutstats.html

Advance programs can be attained through Non-American Dental Association (ADA) approved dental specialties. These are dental implantology, operative dentistry, dental anesthesiology, oral medicine or geriatric/special needs. This residency programs take 1 – 4 years depending on the concurrence of the masters or doctoral degree programs. Some schools offer Advanced Education in General Dentistry (AEGD) or General Practice Residency which take one or two years, https://www.dental.columbia.edu/education/postdoctoral-and-residency-programs/advanced-education-general-dentistry-program-aegd

Note that graduate programs demand that applicants complete a D.M.D. or D.D.S. through a school which is accredited by the Commission on Dental Accreditation https://www.dental.columbia.edu/education/ddsrogram&http://www.ada.org/~/media/CODA/Files/AEGD_Standards.pdf?la=en.

Applicants have a better chance if they possess experiences and abilities in teaching, research and leadership and community activities. Some schools may require you to be eligible to have a full clinical license to undertake a clinical specialty program while others demand for a resident limited license. Visit the following website that assist in the Postdoctoral Dental Matching Program for residency spots. AEGD accommodates highest number of foreign educated dentist.
 https://natmatch.com/dentres/documents/progreg.pdf

Visit the following link to understand the Two-year AEGD program for Internationally Educated Students https://admissions.dental.ufl.edu/iedp/programs-application-process/advanced-education-in-general-dentistry/

4th Option Academic Careers

Academic dentistry is achieved through specialty training in America and pursuit of an advanced standing predoctoral training. Major advantage of choosing this approach as an International Trained specialist is close contact with the recent updates in the field of dentistry, expert and peer influence, exposure in an interdisciplinary environment, close collaboration in a cutting-edge professionalism. Educational loans are also offered. Therefore, it is advantageous for Foreign Trained Dentist need certification from the Commission on Dental Accreditation (CODA). This ensures that you can secure an academic position. Dentist trained in a specialty undergo the Board Certification which is a procedure of intense examinations to demonstrate excellent proficiency in the field of practice.

Commission on Dental Accreditation (CODA) – focuses in the accreditation and constant qualify enhancement of dental education programs as well as their development and implementation.
https://www.ada.org/en/coda

CODA accredited Programs are listed in the following link by state. This link can help you chose your state of interest in terms of practicing https://www.danb.org/The-Dental-Community/Dental-Assistants/Dental-Assisting-Programs/CODA-Accredited-Dental-Assisting-Programs.aspx

Keep in mind that the nature of appointment matters which are in two categories: Tenure and Non-tenure. Academic Dentistry Positions can be viewed through American Dental Education Association this website www.adea.org/dentedjobs.aspx. Faculty position can be viewed in through the academic key website
http://dentistry.academickeys.com/seeker_search.php.

Upon graduating as a Foreign Trained Dentists through the Advanced Standing Dental Program in America makes you automatically eligible for Dental Licensure. This is after passing the required State Specific Licensure Exam. Foreign Trained Dentist who have attained a specialty program are required to achieve a University Specific Faculty Dental Permit to attend patients in Dental Schools Clinics, some dental schools require full dental licensure.

5th Option Private Practice in America

After Completion of a Dental degree from Non-CODA Certified Institution, foreign trained students are required to pursue a pathway to acquire licensure by finalizing an 2-3 years advanced dental degree or alternatively a Degree in one of the Specialty. This is the only option accepted Nationwide which is the attainment of the Advanced standing degree. Only a few states have the mandatory completion of a dental degree and the completion of a clinical specialty program. Initial licensure requirement is determined by the state you are applying for practice.

Optional Training Status can be considered based on your field of study. This can range from 12 months for a degree holder and 30 months for STEM degree holders.

Requirements for private practice include:

• Completion of NBDE 1 & NBDE 11

• Completion of all sections Regional Dental Licensure

• Advanced standing degree (D.M.D. or D.D.S.) from CODA certified school

• or attainment of CODA certified graduate program in one of the approved specialties

• Passing of jurisprudence law and ethics exams

• Background checks, Fingerprint clearance

• Valid legal status

Click to the following link to understand the requirement by state https://www.asdanet.org/index/dental-student-resources/tips-for-international-dental-students

Prerequisite for Foreign Educated Dentist

H1B Visa is a program that allows US based employers to hire foreign Nationals. As a foreign dentist you must

- Attain a post graduate degree in Dentistry, Doctor of Dental Surgery (DDS)

- Pass the National Board Dental Examination

- Possess Licensure of State that you intend to practice

- Copy of the H-1B Petition

- Submission of the Labor Condition Application (LCA/ETA9035)

The **LCA** is mandatory document which potential employer submits with the Employment Training Administration (ETA) when they are seeking to hire non-immigrants in a specific profession for not less than three. It must be authorized by the official pursuant of the Department of Labor

Employment Training Administration an interagency of the US Department which comprises of the National Processing Center (NPC) and the Office of Work Force Security.

Please note that the process of acquiring the legal work visa is an intricate and weighty affair therefore It needs of critical planning for both the foreign educated dentist and the potential employer

Potential Employer must also file a Labor Condition Application through the US department of Labor. This includes the H supplement, Form 1-129 through the USCIS petition for a non-immigrant worker and official LCA by the United States Citizenship and immigration Services (USCIS)

Willing employers can pay $1,225 for filing expenses which may take approximately 15 days

The Legal Permanent Residency or the Green Card allows for you as a Foreign Educated Dentist to work and live in America. Immigrant visas or employment-based green will accommodate most of the dentists. Dentists will fall under the two categories

- E-B2 category - mainly caters foreign educated professional that possess Advanced Degrees such as DDS (more than four-year bachelor's degree + Inclusive of 5 years' experience).

- E-B3 category – covers for foreign national professionals and skilled employees. Dentists fall under the umbrella of professionals since they possess a US baccalaureate degree or having a foreign equivalent.

After your petition has been approved, booking the H-IB visa interview is the next step. You will need to do this through the Department of State Website in collaboration with the closest American Embassy or consulate. The process is as follows:

• On the Department of State website, the form DS-160 is to be filled.

• On the confirmation form a 10-digit bard code will be feature that is necessary for the securing the appointment for the interview.

• After scheduling the appointment fees ($1,225) should be paid and two appointments scheduled 1) for the offsite facilitation center and 2) with the consulate or embassy. This should be done within a minimum two days after the submission of request.

Upon passing the consulate interview it is time to plan your relocation process since all documents are in order. Education programs and the visa programs are major avenues that offer a chance for Dentist to work in America since they are categorized as Professionals. However, agents like in the case of Nursing professional are not used to recruit Dentists

Dentistry as a Lucrative Career

Salary scale depends also on the state that you have applied to practice in

Follow this link for a comparison of Dentists salary by state

Salary by State: http://salarybystate.org/tag/best-paying-states-for-dentists

US Bureau of Labor Statistics:
http://www.bls.gov/oes/current/oes291021.htm

Transitioning to America as a Foreign Trained Pharmacist

I have had the privilege of interacting closely with pharmacists in the United States. As a Foreign educated pharmacist, you may compete for a limited number of positions which will greatly depend on polices of the institution as well as the state you desire to work in. Private pharmacy institutions offer more chances to International Graduates within the programs as compared to state supported or public institutions. Therefore, as foreign educated pharmacist, it is mandatory to meet the equivalent or minimum requirements as American students. This includes course bonuses and standardized tests.

Step One: Education Qualification

As a foreign educated pharmacist who desires to practice in America you must have;

• Graduated from an accredited school / institution of pharmacy

• Present Documentation that you are licensed

• And or registered for practice as a pharmacist in foreign country or jurisdiction

• **Preceding to 1 January 2003** - Applicants issued a pharmacy degree prior to this date must have completed a four-year pharmacy program (minimum) by the time of graduation.

• **On or after 1 January 2003** - Applicants issued a pharmacy degree on or after this date must have completed a five-year pharmacy program (minimum) by the time of graduation

• Pre-Pharmacy course achieved in the University Level maybe considered for evaluation as part of the candidate's education achievement.

Step Two: Evaluation of Credentials

This process requires that you apply to the Education Credentials Evaluators with the objective of evaluating your foreign credentials. As a foreign undergraduate your training will be assessed in order to ensure that you are equally educated as an individual practicing pharmacy in the United States.

The Education Credentials Evaluators necessitates that you produce two copies of the following documents

• Official Transcript of University attended

• Proof of Degree Certificate

• Translation of non-English Documents

• Proof of A or O levels or equivalent (Depending on Country of Origin)

• Fee for the General Evaluation Report

At this point it is advisable that you check out the National Association of Boards of Pharmacy to see what they recommend. The following are the report types and fees. It is highly recommended that you consult the institution you are applying to find type of report that is required.

General Report: $85

This report is used for Immigration, Employment, Military and professional licensure purposes. It includes each educational credential equivalent to that of the US.

General with Grade Average Report: $110

This report is used for further education. It includes each educational credential equivalent to that of the US and Grade average of each university level credential

Course by Course Report: $160

Used for further education which includes high school college or university, Professional licensure and employment follow this link for the details which will be included in the report https://www.ece.org/ECE/Individuals/Services--Fees

High School and University Level Course-by-Course Report: $195

Used for Further education high school college or university

Subject Analysis: $210

Timeline of delivery of reports 3 business days via FedEx

For Foreign Transcript Evaluation Services, the World Education Services, Inc offers evaluation reports

Education Evaluation Reports

Course by Course Evaluation

WES ICAP - $205

WES Basic - $160

Please follow this link for further insight on extra fees

https://www.wes.org/evaluations-and-fees/education/transfer-admissions/

Professional License or Certification Reports

Course by Course Evaluation

WES ICAP - $205

WES Basic - $160

Time line of process – 7 business days for receipt of request

Please follow this link for further insight on extra fees

https://www.wes.org/evaluations-and-fees/professional-license-certification/medicine/

Professional Licenses or Certification

Please note, at this point you must make a request to the ECE to forward a copy of the General Evaluation Report to the FPGEC and include the Supporting educational documents.

All official documents are to be submitted to the FPGEC in a sealed envelope to the issuing body.

Please visit

https://www.ece.org/ECE/Individuals/Professional-Licensure-Reports/NABP for NABP documentation requirements

Step 3: Foreign Pharmacy Graduate Examination Committee: Certification Application

You will need to create an online account/e-Profile which will generate am e-profile ID. The e-profile ID acts as an identifier for the FPGEC Program and used in requesting services from the Pearson VUE or NABP.

This process calls for a non-refundable application fee of $100 and evaluation fee of $450

After submission of the application you are required to send the following via postal mail to NABP:

• 2 identical full-face passport sized photographs

• Licensure or registration as pharmacist from country of practice

• Photos of Certified copies of current identification such as passport, Driving License, Identification Card

Foreign Pharmacy Graduate Equivalency Examination (FPGEE) is an exam that is offered twice a year, which is part of the FPGEC programs. It is administered through the Pearson VUE test sites.

Refer to this link to gain more knowledge on how to prepare, schedule, register and take the FPGEE test https://nabp.pharmacy/programs/fpgee/

FPGEC Application Bulletin indicates the requirements that should be met to have the FPGEC certification. This includes having the FPGEE identification card

Foreign Pharmacy Graduate Examination Committee requires that Foreign graduated pharmacist achieve FPGEC certification prior to application for licensures from the State board of Pharmacy.

National Association of Boards of Pharmacy ensures the provision of public health safety though transfer of Pharmacist licensure and development and implementation of pharmacist competence evaluation programs.

Further resources

https://nabp.pharmacy/wp-content/uploads/2018/08/FPGEC-Application-Bulletin-August-27-2018.pdf

Step 4: Language Proficiency Test - TOEFL iBT

The FPGEC certification Program requires that you take the Test of English as a Foreign Language (TOEFL) Internet-Based Test (iBT)

This test is taken at an educational Testing Service test center which is located within the NABP member jurisdiction.

TOEFL iBTis taken any time during the EPGEC certification process

Pass rates of the FPGEC certification are:

1. Reading: 22

2. Listening: 21

3. Speaking: 26

4. Writing: 24

Step 5: Internship

After meeting the above requirements and successful results you can register for an internship programs with the state of choice. Majority of the States require that you complete at least 1500 Hrs. of practice. This means you seek out a pharmacist who will act as a preceptor in your internship facility and register as a pharmacist intern with the State Board Pharmacy. After completion of the internship, the NABP in collaboration with the State pharmacy authorizes to the NAPLEX and MPJE.

Once the hourly requirement is met, apply for the North American Pharmacy Licensure Examination (NAPLEX) and Multistate Jurisprudence Pharmacy Examination (MJPE)

Refer to this resource to understand the requirements of licensure by state http://2hqyh93y2sj32lqbnw40aoj0.wpengine.netdna-cdn.com/wp-content/uploads/000384251.pdf

North American Pharmacy Licensure Examination is a computer administered exam evaluates the applicant's knowledge in the pharmacy field and the ability to practice. It's a among of the many components of licensure requirements by the boards of pharmacy as part of the evaluation of the graduate's competences to practice as a pharmacy

Exam Fee - $ 485

Details are in the following link on how to apply for the NAPLEX exam http://naplexexam.com/naplex-exam-eligibility.html

Multistate Jurisprudence Pharmacy Examination (MJPE) this exam is formulated through combination of federal and state questions to test the pharmacy jurisprudence knowledge of prospective. It acts as a pharmacy law examination in the participating jurisdictions and test an applicant's mastery of the pharmacy law. Remember this differs based on the state police and ethics of practice

For further information on how to apply and schedule the Multistate Jurisprudence Pharmacy Examination follow

https://nabp.pharmacy/programs/mpje/

Step 5: Visa Application and Screening

H-1B is acquired for both internship programs and the licensed pharmacist positions

Requirements:

You must prove that you have equivalent education in comparison to American Pharmacy Graduates

Potential employer must show that you as a foreign employee is qualified possessing a PharmD Degree or a Bachelor's degree in pharmacy, must also show that you are licensed in the state that you want to practice

Other alternative is the application of the Labor Certification Green Cards in the EB2 or EB3 Categories

Transitioning as a Foreign Trained Medical Doctor in America

A former professional colleague decided his need for research and technological innovation could not be accommodated outside the United States. When he heard there is a possibility to migrate and become a doctor in the United States, he was thrilled with this possibility. With some help and a very stringent and arduous process he managed to come to the United States, where he is legally practicing medicine. Through the experiences of my medical doctor friends, I have seen the process they went through to successfully start working and make money as medical doctors in the United States. The trick for foreign doctors is to choose residency programs wisely. Keep in mind that some residency programs are very competitive.

For instance, Orthopedics, Emergency medicine, Dermatology and Plastic Surgery are very competitive compared to Internal medicine, Family Medicine, Pediatric Medicine and Psychiatry. If you have a passion for pursuing competitive residency programs, your examination scores and personal statements should be among the best. Remember to use review courses while preparing for examinations. When looking for residency programs consider applying in rural and underserved areas to lessen the competition. Make sure to apply to as many residency programs as possible.

Consider working in underserved communities and focus on less competitive residency programs to improve your chances of admission. Student loan repayment programs can be available in underserved areas unlike big cities where programs have more than enough applicants. Make sure to understand the mission statement for each medical program. Another popular option for immigrants is that they get student loan repayments and Citizenship opportunities by serving in the US Military. Many foreign trained medical residents work for the Department of Veteran Affairs (VA) which is a Federal government entity. Working with the government might come in handy if you consider waiving the stringent requirement for J1 visa. More on J1 visa on page 102.

Foreign Professional Doctors also known as International Medical Graduates (IMG) who desire to acquire licensure as physicians in the America can do so through the National Resident Program. This is the foremost channel which ensures completion of a Residency Hospital program. This is achieved through The National Resident Program is Non-Governmental organization that ensures medical graduates are placed and have the opportunities of training programs in the American Based Hospitals for the U.S and Non-U. S based students (http://www.nrmp.org/). However, as an IMG the following criteria will be met prior to seeking a residency program

Step 1: Credential Requirements – Medical Requirements

• 4 Years Academic Credit

• Enrollment

• Transfer of Credit

• Should have studied in an accredited medical school by the World Federation of Medical Education which ensures Global Criteria for medical education

• Listing of Appropriate credentials, School of graduation and year of graduation in the International Medical Education Directory (IMED)

• Verification by the Educational Commission for Foreign Medical Graduates (ECFMG)

• Pass the residency training program

• Eligibility for licensure and practice in the country of origin

The above the requirements ensures that the Foreign Medial Graduates are certified by the Educational Commission for Foreign Medical Students (ECFMG). To attain licensure from the ECFMG as a Foreign medical graduate you must undertake and pass the United States Medical Licensing Examination (USMLE). Exams by USMLE are in three categories whose objective is to evaluate your abilities in the vast spectrum of knowledge, medical concepts and principles to assess the physician's basic patient focused skills.

The exams are as follows

• Assessment 1 – Basic integral science concepts tied with clinical scenarios

• Assessment 2 – a) Clinical Knowledge evaluates clinical science

b) Clinical skills hands on evaluation of communication skills and gathering of information and physical examination of patients

• Assessment 3 - Application of medical knowledge and the application of clinical science and biomedical essentials

Kindly be advised that the ECFMG will not consider you application complete if your credentials are not verified and received directly from the medical school. Required credentials are final medical school transcript and medical diploma.

USMLE evaluates the attributes of the physician in the application if concepts, knowledge, principles and key patient centered skills. The three steps evaluation complement each other with the goal ensuring medical readiness for medical licensure. https://www.usmle.org/about/

Step 2: ECFMG Certification and Credential evaluation

As a Foreign Medical graduate who desires to practice in the United States you need to be issued a Standard ECFMG Certificate. This Certificate is offered to you when all the medical education and examinations requirements are met. Refer to https://www.ecfmg.org/#

ECFMG Certification ensures that a foreign medical graduate secures entry into an accredited Graduate Medical Program (GME) in the United States

Certification includes:

• Name of applicant

• USMLE/ECFMG identification number of Applicant

• Dates when the examination requirements were taken

• Date when certificate was issued

• Dates of exams passed (passed through performance) which remain valid with the objective of entry into the GME

Fees for ECFMG Certification is $125

Examinations: Assessment 1 $190

Assessment 2 CK - $910

Assessment 2 CS – $1,565

Please investigate other fees under the following link

https://www.ecfmg.org/fees/index.html

Step 3: Credential evaluation also known as the Certification Verification Service (CVS) is carried out by the ECFMG. The ECFMG approves status of certification of you as an International/foreign medical graduate which offers two types of reports a status and confirmation report

https://www.ecfmg.org/cvs/reports.html

The https://www.ecfmg.org/cvs/index.html link offers the Certification Verification Service which is done by filling an online form

https://www.ecfmg.org/cvs/forms.html

Certification Verification Service - $45

Step 4: Residency Program

After attaining the ECFMG certification, as an Internationally educated physician you must complete a residency training program that is accredited. Duration of the residency program will be at least 3 years. This is regardless of previous completion of previous residency programs in country of origin.

To qualify for this option, the medical graduate must have a visa approved to carry out their residency program in the United States. It is therefore highly recommended that the Foreign Graduate shares in the observer ship rotation in a clinical setting prior to applying for the residency program (https://www.ama-assn.org/life-career/observership-program-listings-international-medical-graduates). Advantage of this approach is that the international medical graduate will be exposed and familiar with the clinical practice settings and chance to meet with physicians who can be sued as strong references when it comes to the application process of the residency program. Majority of the programs require that you apply via the Electronic Residency Application Service, the ECFMG harmonizes this process.

Selection of the Residency Program can be approached from through four major ways:

• Preliminary Programs: they are 1-year programs if you wish to specialize and you require a year of internal medial training.

• Transitional Programs where you will rotate 1st year residents through different hospitals every 2-3moths. Note transitional programs are equated as 1 year of training thus they may not offer enough credits to move to the next year of training.

• Categorized Programs this are considered as traditional or hospital based which go for three years. They allow the residents to train or attain the boards eligibility if your performance is satisfactory

• Primary Care Programs focus on ambulatory care experience in the communities. This program is becoming more and more common in the medical filed. The primary care programs are highly advised for graduates who want to practice as generalist

To secure a Medical residency International Graduates as a graduate you are encouraged to submit to at least 25 programs. This will increase chances of being absorbed or matched in a residency program.

Various residency programs require that you as an IMG apply via the Electronic Residency Application Service (ERAS) which is offered by ECFMG https://www.ecfmg.org/2019ib/eras.html

Fees

• ECFMG Token Fee: $120

• USMLE Transcript Fee: $80

• NRMP Matching Fee: $85 extra fees based on categories are indicated in the following link https://www.ecfmg.org/eras/timeline.html

Fees depend greatly on the number of programs applied for per Specialty

Programs Per Specialty >> Fees

Minimum of 10 >> $99

11-20 >> $14 each

21-30 >> $18 each

31 and more >> $26 each

Information source https://students-residents.aamc.org/applying-residency/article/fees-eras-residency-applications/

Process for residency application:

• Presentation of application free of grammatical errors. Application should be original

• On the Curriculum Vitae Underscore Unique qualifications, academic based experiences, volunteer work and test scores

• Acquire solid experience in US based health care facility before application of residency. This will be an advantage due to strong letters of recommendations

• Make certain of the application NRMP Number should be correct if registered for the Match

• Preparation with regards to immigration and visa status

The following link indicates the timeline for the residency matching https://www.aamc.org/cim/residency/application/applying/337902/matchtimeline.html

Step 5: Meeting the Immigration Requirements

Visa that allows for clinical training for International Medical Graduates with the objective of offering medical services is known as the J-1 Visa. The US department of State authorizes the ECFMG to sponsor foreign physicians the J-1 visa.

Following criteria must be met
• Passing of the USMLE Step 1 and Step CK
• Valid ECFMG certificate
• Possess contract or official letter offering you a position in a program either for Training with a medical school or Graduate Medical Education

• Deliver statement f need from Ministry of Health from country of last permanent resident

Home Country Physical Presence Requirement

Upon finishing the training in the U.S the graduate, you must return to your country of origin for a period of two years to offer the knowledge gained while training in the US. This obligation must be met by the J-1 visa holders prior to be being eligible for U.S visa adjustment. These visas are

• L–Intra-company transferee

• H–Temporary worker

• U.S.–Permanent resident

However, you can be exempted from the home residence if you receive a waiver. Circumstances that can warrant a waiver are

i. Demonstration or proof that you will suffer persecution in mother country or country of last permanent residence

ii. Attainment of the residency program will prove to be having exceptional hardship to applicant's family or spouse who are either permanent residents of U.S

iii. Employment by the Interested Government Agency whose interest is continued employment of the physician in America

The second option is the H-1B visa which caters for skilled/workers who have earned professional level degrees. This allows foreign nationals to gain professional employment for up to 6 years. This is available for you as a foreign medical graduate if you have passed the required exams, licensure as required by the state you want to practice in and possession of an unrestricted license to practice medicine and must have graduated from a US or foreign medical school

Third option is the Immigrant visa also known as the green card or permanent visa status which allows individuals to work and live in the U.S.

Step 5: License to Practice

Licensure must be applied for the State intended for practice. This is done after completion of 1-3 years of practicing medicine outside the United States. Despite the differing requirements by state for practicing licenses, all states have the standard requirement of proof of education appropriate training and completion of the exam licensure.

It is therefore important to ask for a copy of licensure requirements of the state they intend to practice in and the time frame used to process the application of the Practice License.

https://commerce.ama-assn.org/store/catalog/productDetail.jsp?product_id=prod2420007 this link offers you the e-book State Medical Licensure Requirements and Statistics which costs $90. It offers the current information on requirement of licensure and statistics in America.

Transitioning as a foreign Physical Therapist to America

The little-known secret is that you can get a green card if you are a qualified Physical Therapist. With a significant number of people in the United States transiting into the elderly bracket, others getting injured and disabled. The need for foreign physiotherapists has really gone up. Through my articles and weekly vlogs, I have recognized people asking how they can come to the United States as physiotherapists and this prompted my research. The findings have led to the following process log that would be of great help to anyone who would want to come to the United States as a physiotherapist.

As a Foreign Educated Physiotherapist with the desire to work in the United States your ambition will be determined by a few factors such as the Level of education you have acquired in your country, the process of document evaluation and licensure. These processes are also greatly influenced by the Foreign Credentialing Commission on Physical Therapy.

Foreign Credentialing Commission on Physical Therapy (FCCPT) supports foreign trained therapist who desire to practice in the United States. As an agency it offers evaluations that are accepted in the 53 jurisdictions within America. It is the only dedicated institution that assess and review documents in the process of licensure an immigration http://www.fccpt.org/

Education requirements

• Master's Degree or Higher in Physiotherapy and a

• Minimum of 202.1 semester credits

Assuming, that already you have attained the above educational requirements, two things will follow. That is determining the type of visa required

and which State in America you would like to practice in. Please remember that each state has its independent prerequisites for health care professionals who wish to practice under them. Each State has a licensure board that outline the requirements to be met kindly visit the following link for further information: Licensing Authorities Contact Information
http://www.fsbpt.org/FreeResources/LicensingAuthoritiesContactInformation.aspx

Credential Evaluation Process

This process involves four steps

• Appropriate institution will be requested to provide the original academic documents

• Authentication and verification of the received documents

• Document evaluation

• Compilation of an electronic summary report sent to you and the licensure agency

After application and paying necessary fees, submit forms authorizing the schools and agencies to submit your documents to the FCCPT (FCCPT uses ORIGINAL DCOUMENTS ONLY). At this point they will be assessed if they are authentic and this may take up to 8 weeks.

During this process the Coursework Tool (CWT) is used to determine if level of education acquired is equal to that of the US-PT (it compares content and credits). Kindly follow this link to understand how the Coursework tools acts as a guide in the evaluation of PT foreign educated physical therapists
https://www.fsbpt.org/FreeResources/RegulatoryResources/CourseworkTools(CWT).aspx and
https://www.fsbpt.org/FreeResources/CredentialingOrganizationsforNonUSCandidates.aspx

This step is critical since it determines if you are qualified for the Health Care workers Type 1 Certificate (HCWC) for Immigration by the USCIS. The U.S. Citizenship and Immigration Services requires that foreign educated Physical Therapist MUST have an equivalent of a First Professional

Degree based on the most current type of CWT. The other agency is CGFNS Please visit

http://www.cgfns.org/services/certification/visascreen-visa-credentials-assessment/

CGFNS FEES Visa Screen Application $540

Expedited Review Service $500 Timeline 5 business days

Finally, the evaluation process will offer a comprehensive report which compares the applicant's educational threshold, licensure requirements based on jurisdiction and areas of deficiency.

The following agencies are licensed to use the CWT

• Foreign Credentialing Commission on Physical Therapy (FCCPT)

• CGFNS for use by International Consultants of Delaware (ICD

• University of Texas at Austin

• International Credentialing Associates

• International Education Research Foundation (IERF)

Note each state has differing and additional requirements. The Federation of State Boards of Physical Therapy (FSBPT) offers detailed information of licensure requirements based on jurisdiction. Please follow http://www.fsbpt.org/RegulatoryTools/ReferenceGuide/index.asp, http://www.fsbpt.org/FreeResources/ForeignEducatedPTsandPTAssistan ts/ImmigrationInformation.aspx and

Visa requirements

For you to acquire employment permits as Foreign PT, the U.S. Citizenship and Immigration Services requires you to complete an evaluation. This evaluation is known as Type 1 comprehensive review which covers the following areas:

• Educational Documents

• Eligibility to practice in mother country or country in which you completed studies or evaluation of current held licenses

• English Proficiency test: Internet Based TOEFL (TOEFL iBT) where a score of 63 is required in Composite of reading comprehension, listening comprehension and writing and a score of 26 in speaking.

Since the USCIS considers you as Health Care Professional you are required to obtain a Health care worker certification (HCWC) before obtaining a visa. The following types of visa require the HCWC:

• H-1B allows potential US based employers to temporarily employ foreign workers in fields that require at least a bachelor's degrees or higher. The foreign worker can enter the US under this visa and live for 3 year with a possible extension of 6 years.

• EB2 allows permanent workers holding an advanced degree with the objective of employment. Advantage of this visa is that the holder is permitted to apply for the green card (Permanent status)

• EB3 allows for a permanent worker with skilled or professional competencies for employment in the United States. Holder of this visa permitted to apply for the green card

Please visit this link for additional information
http://www.fsbpt.org/FreeResources/ForeignEducatedPTsandPTAssistants/ImmigrationInformation.aspx

It is therefore recommended that you

• Identify your immigration needs, that where you desire to work and live

• Understand the requirements for the type of credential assessment needing to be completed

• Research and understand the requirements of the state that you desire to work in. It is also good to compare states for further insight

• Compile all documents that are required

• Starting early is key since there may be delays may be in evaluation process or receipt of documents

The US Bureau of Labor Statistics indicates that 2017 median salary of PT's was $86,850 at $41.76 per hour. Job outlook as of 2016 was expected to be on the rise at the rate of 28% between the year 2016-2026.

Salary scale depends on which setting you are working in this can be either of the following

- Nursing and residential Care facilities $92,000

- Home Healthcare Services $93,000

- Hospitals $89,000

- Offices of physical occupational speech therapist audiologist 83,000

California, Texas New York Florida and Illinois have the highest employment levels of Physiotherapist with a salary ranging from $95,000-$90,000

Transitioning Careers: Learn about how to make money with various occupations and their requirements

Feedback from my social media platforms and website, led me to delve into many other professions apart from the medical field that would enable one to migrate to the United States. The following is a compilation of skilled and semi-skilled labor that is required in the United States and how one can come in as a foreigner and work in the various fields and industries.

Farming, Fishing, and Forestry in The United States

Farming, fishing, and forestry occupations is one of the lowest paid occupational groups, with a median annual wage of $23,510 compared to the median annual wage for all occupations of $37,040.

Employment in farming, fishing, and forestry occupations is projected to show little or no change over the next few years. Projected increases in some agricultural worker occupations will be offset by declines in logging occupations.

Agricultural Workers

Agricultural workers maintain crops and tend to livestock. They perform physical labor and operate machinery under the supervision of farmers, ranchers, and other agricultural managers.

Farmers, Ranchers, and Other Agricultural Managers

Farmers, ranchers, and other agricultural managers operate establishments that produce crops, livestock, and dairy products.

Fishing and Hunting Workers

Fishing and hunting workers catch and trap various types of animal life. The fish and wild animals they catch are for human food, animal feed, bait, and other uses.

Forest and Conservation Workers

Forest and conservation workers measure and improve the quality of forests. Under the supervision of foresters and forest and conservation technicians, they develop, maintain, and protect forests.

Logging Workers

Logging workers harvest thousands of acres of forests each year. The timber they harvest provides the raw material for many consumer goods and industrial products.

Additional Farming, Fishing, and Forestry Occupations

Agricultural Inspectors

Agricultural Inspectors inspect agricultural commodities, processing equipment and facilities, and fish and logging operations in order to ensure compliance with regulations and laws governing health, quality, and safety.

Farm Labor Contractors

Farm labor contractors recruit and hire seasonal or temporary agricultural laborers. May transport, house, and provide meals for workers.

First-Line Supervisors of Farming, Fishing, and Forestry Workers

First-Line Supervisors of Farming, Fishing, and Forestry Workers directly supervise and coordinate the activities of agricultural, forestry, aqua cultural, and related workers.

Forest and Conservation Technicians

Forest and Conservation Technicians provide technical assistance regarding the conservation of soil, water, forests, or related natural resources.

Graders and Sorters (Agricultural Products)

Graders and Sorters (Agricultural Products) grade, sort, or classify unprocessed food and other agricultural products by size, weight, color, or condition.

Building and maintenance careers

Building maintenance workers can find jobs without formal training, but education and training in areas such as plumbing, dry walling, electrical wiring and flooring can be helpful when seeking comprehensive 'handymen' jobs. A balanced combination of classroom learning and hands-on experience gives aspiring maintenance workers the knowledge needed to handle various structural, electrical and HVAC (heating, ventilating and air conditioning) issues that can arise in buildings.

At least some training in basic wiring and plumbing installation and repair is needed for building maintenance jobs. Additional coursework in HVAC systems, mechanical principles, carpentry, refrigeration systems, tool maintenance and welding are recommended to round out one's knowledge of this field. Classes in mathematics, general construction and safety are also useful. Many of these skills are taught individually within certificate or diploma programs but can be learned collectively in through a degree program.

Licensure requirements for building maintenance professionals vary from state to state and are commonly needed for those working in the specialty areas of plumbing and electrical work. Although not required for employment, a variety of certifications are also available for building maintenance professionals to demonstrate their skill level and maintenance proficiencies.

The most widely accepted certifications are offered through the International Maintenance Institute (IMI).

The IMI offers the certified maintenance technician credential at three different levels as well as designations as a certified maintenance professional or certified maintenance manager. IMI certifications are valid for two years and require several continuing education credits for renewal.

As technology advances, so do the computerized control systems installed in newer buildings to control building temperatures, timed lighting schedules, and energy efficiency. Because of this, there is a growing need for building maintenance professionals to develop basic computer skills in order to navigate through computer-controlled equipment. Building maintenance workers should also be able to perform physical tasks, possess manual dexterity, and be able to perform basic mathematical operations.

Building maintenance training programs come in two forms, as building maintenance certificates and facilities management certificates. Through these programs, students can learn various methods for maintaining and repairing the essential systems of a building, as well as prepare themselves for licensure, certification, and additional professional development during their careers.

What General Maintenance and Repair Workers Do

General maintenance and repair workers fix and maintain machines, mechanical equipment, and buildings. They paint, repair flooring, and work on plumbing, electrical, and air-conditioning and heating systems, among other tasks.

General maintenance and repair workers often carry out many different tasks in a single day. They could work at any number of indoor or outdoor locations. They may work inside a single building, such as a hotel or hospital, or be responsible for the maintenance of many buildings, such as those in an apartment complex or on a college campus.

Jobs in this occupation typically require a high school diploma or equivalent. General maintenance and repair workers often learn their skills on the job for several years. They start out performing simple tasks while watching and learning from skilled maintenance workers.

The median annual wage for general maintenance and repair workers was $37,670 in May 2017.

Construction

Individuals who are interested in becoming contractors often learn the skills of the trade through hands-on training and working on a construction site. Before becoming a contractor, many people have a job as a laborer. Apprenticeships and internships provide valuable training in carpentry, plumbing, electrical work or masonry, and can sometimes substitute for an education background.

It is more common to have a bachelor's degree to work as a contractor, and many accredited colleges and universities offer programs in construction science, construction management, building science or civil engineering, according to the U.S. Bureau of Labor Statistics (BLS) (www.bls.gov). These programs focus on various aspects of the construction business, including classes in site planning, designing, construction methods, contract administration, building codes and standards, as well as mathematics, accounting and information technology.

Master's degree programs are also available at many institutions in construction management or construction science. Some construction professionals seek out bachelor's or master's degrees in business administration or finance as well. Those with master's degrees in this field often become contractors at larger construction or construction management companies due to their credentials, as reported by the BLS.

While certification is not required to work in construction management, it is becoming more common because it shows competence and demonstrates the proper training in the field. Certification opportunities are available at the American Institute of Constructors and the Construction Management Association of America, according to the BLS.

The American Institute of Constructors offers the Associate Constructor (AC) and Certified Professional Constructor (CPC) designations to those who meet the requirements and successfully complete the proper examinations. The Construction Management Association of America awards the Certified Construction Manager (CCM) designation to workers who have the required experience and pass a technical examination.

Applicants can improve their ability to compete for jobs by completing a bachelor's degree in construction management or construction science and acquiring a state license.

Most employers require construction and building inspectors to have at least a high school diploma and work experience in construction trades. Inspectors also typically learn on the job. Many states and local jurisdictions require some type of license or certification.

The median annual wage for construction and building inspectors was $59,090 in May 2017. $28.41 per hour

Production

A career as in manufacturing can be pursued with a high school diploma or GED. Experience using tools is typically required, and those who enter this field will have to complete workplace safety courses and other training through their employer.

The manufacturing industry is a diversified field that includes jobs ranging from production workers to purchasing agents. The top two occupations in manufacturing are team assemblers and machinists. The third most populous occupation, which may be thought of as quality control employees, includes inspectors, testers, sorters, samplers and weighers.

Required Education High school diploma or GED

Other Requirements On-the-job training and voluntary certifications available

Median Salary $40,550 annually for machinists

Source: *U.S. Bureau of Labor Statistics

Manufacturing Career Options

Team assemblers

Team assemblers fabricate or construct products on an assembly line. In order to respond to demand shifts, these workers rotate on different assignments throughout the production process. By doing this, they become well-versed in all stages of assembly and are able to adjust to worker absences and supply chain issues. Team assemblers may also be responsible for quickly scanning parts, removing faulty parts and determining the source of a defect.

As reported by the U.S. Bureau of Labor Statistics (BLS), employment growth for assemblers and fabricators is projected to decline one percent from 2014 to 2024. This job decline is due to an increase in productivity with fewer workers in many manufacturing companies. In May 2015, the BLS stated that team assemblers earned a median annual salary of $29,080.

Machinists

Machinists use specialized tools, including computer numerically controlled (CNC) machines, to create or assemble parts, mechanisms and products. Machinists begin by consulting blueprints or instructional guides to determine the equipment to use and actions to take. These professionals then perform the required work and follow-up by inspecting products for structural integrity and accuracy to specifications.

Machinists could see ten percent employment growth between 2014 and 2024, according to the BLS. A continuing need for machinists despite advances in technologies is expected. As of May 2015, the BLS says, machinists earned a median yearly salary of $40,550.

Inspectors, Testers, Sorters, Samplers and Weighers

This group ensures quality control by checking products for specification and functional conformance. This may include verifying weights and measures, as well as testing and sending back defects. Additional duties may include reviewing products for durability and fixing minor problems.

The BLS indicates that as of May 2015, 508,590 employed inspectors, testers, sorters, samplers and weighers earned a median annual salary of $36,000. Employment for quality control inspectors, which includes those that inspect manufacturing equipment and products, is expected to see no job growth during the 2014-2024 decade.

Requirements

Prospective candidates may enter the manufacturing field after completing high school. These new hires may receive on-the-job training on handling power tools, assembling parts and using specific quality-control instruments to verify dimensions. Additionally, new employees may participate in employer-sponsored classroom assignments on topics ranging from occupational safety to assembly line controls.

Some positions may ask for postsecondary education. For example, inspectors may benefit from having earned a certificate in computer-aided design. These 6-12-month programs may include instruction on design setup, scaling and modification. Similarly, machinists may be required to have completed a 2-year associate's degree program or 4-year apprenticeship. Apprentices may receive training on reading mechanical drawings, setting up equipment and operating specialized machinery, such as CNC machines.

Sales

Rewarding sales careers are found in just about every industry. Employees realize a strong sales team often leads to a successful company. Many companies make hiring skilled sales professionals a top priority.

Many professionals choose a sales career for personal satisfaction, freedom from the office, growth and high-income potential. Sales people are paid for their performance.

Hard work and a successful sale record often lead to a promotion such as gaining more prestigious customers, a sales executive trainer position or a sales manager job.

Many of the high paying sales jobs require a higher level of knowledge. Sales people in the low earning sales jobs typically sell a product, whereas sales people in the high earning sales positions typically sell a solution.

Sales careers often require an appropriate education, training, experience, knowledge as well as good interpersonal skills. Some sales jobs involving scientific and technical products require a bachelor degree. However, some sales jobs don't require postsecondary education.

Many companies require beginning sales representatives to participate in a formal training program which can take up to two years to complete.

Different Sales Careers:
• Advertising Sales Agents

• Insurance Sales Agents

• Real Estate Brokers and Sales Agents

- Sales Engineers
- Securities, Commodities and Financial Services Sales Agents
- Travel Agents
- Wholesale and Manufacturing Sales Representatives

Advertising Sales Agents

An advertising sales agent career can technically begin with a high school diploma or proven sales experience; however, some employers prefer applicants with a bachelor degree in Marketing, Communication, Business, or Advertising. Most advertising sales agents receive on-the-job training.

Insurance Sales Agents

People interested in an insurance sales agent career typically need at least a high school diploma, although a growing number of agents now have a Bachelor of Business, Economics, Finance, or a related degree. Upon hire, insurance sales agents typically shadow an experienced insurance sales agent to receive on-the-job training.

Insurance sales agents need to have a license in every state they work. Agents selling life and health insurance and property and casualty insurance must obtain separate licenses. Most state licenses require the insurance sales agent to take continuing education courses every two years.

Insurance sales agents may obtain voluntary certifications demonstrating expertise in specific areas.

Some insurance sales agents opt to become certified to sell additional financial planning services in order to meet consumer demand. Insurance sales agents can obtain these additional certifications through the National Association of Securities Dealers (NASD) which includes the Series 6 exam (for selling only mutual funds and variable annuities), and the Series 7 exam, which qualifies the individual as a general securities sale's representative.

Insurance sales agents must know their product inside out, as they must clearly explain it to potential customers, knowledgably answer any questions, and make helpful suggestions as to which policy to select or any policy changes a customer should make. An Insurance sales agent career includes helping customers with the claim process.

Insurance sales representatives may advance in their career to a managerial position after obtaining experience and perhaps additional education.

Essential Career Information

Education requirement: High school diploma or equivalent

2017 median pay $49,710

(source: Bureau of labor statistics)

Food and beverages

Many food preparation jobs are entry-level jobs in the culinary industry, however some jobs are at a higher level. Typically, people don't need a degree to enter the food preparation industry, however, professionals seeking a food preparation career may benefit from completing a culinary program.

Food preparation employees take care of routine tasks such as slicing vegetables, slicing meats and measuring ingredients. Food preparation workers also make sure they work in a clean environment.

Many employers seek food preparation workers with at least a high school diploma. Most food preparation workers receive on-the-job training.

Quick facts regarding food and beverages and other related workers

2017 Median Pay: $20,410 per year

$9.81 per hour

Typical Entry-Level Education: No formal educational credential

Work Experience in a Related Occupation: None

On-the-job Training: Short-term on-the-job training

Food and beverages careers

• Bartenders

• Chefs and Head Cooks

• Food Service Managers

Bartenders

Typically, to enter a bartender career, workers need to be 18 and older and complete short-term on-the-job training. There are no educational requirements required for a bartender career. However, people who desire to work at higher end restaurants or establishments need more experience and some vocational training.

Training programs include teaching bartenders about customer service, cocktail recipes, state and local laws, how to deal with difficult or unruly patrons, teamwork and proper food procedures.

Chefs and Head Cooks

Typically, people need a high school diploma, formal training from a technical, culinary arts school or community college and experience to enter a head cook career. Some chefs learn skills through apprenticeships or in the armed forces.

Culinary programs and vocational schools offer classes under experienced chefs in areas including food sanitation procedures, kitchen work, menu planning and purchasing/inventory methods. Many programs require head cooks to gain real world kitchen experience through apprenticeships. Associations such as culinary institutes, and trade unions and the U.S. Department of Labor sponsor apprenticeships; they typically last for about two years.

Food Service Managers

Individuals typically do not need a college degree to begin a food service management career. However, increasingly employers seek candidates with some postsecondary education and training. Many food service management companies and national restaurant chains recruit at college hospitality and food management programs. Technical schools and community colleges provide training for individuals interested in a food service manager career.

Most certification and degree programs offer work-study training as well as classes in areas such as nutrition and food preparation, business management and computer science. In addition, restaurant chains and food management companies, such as healthcare food service management, offer intensive training programs. These programs include food preparation, nutrition, employee management and education on company procedures.

Food services managers don't need certification; however, the National Restaurant Association Educational Foundation offers the Foodservice Management Professional (FMP) certificate to recognize outstanding professional service of food service managers.

Mathematics and computing

Rewarding mathematics jobs are available in an array of companies and organizations. A postsecondary education in mathematics provides a variety of career paths. Most math careers go far beyond just crunching numbers, they're challenging, interesting and provide a good salary.

Some careers focus on mathematical research and education, whereas others use mathematics and its applications to build and improve work in finance, sciences, manufacturing, business, engineering and communications. Some mathematicians work in fields such as climate study, astronomy and space exploration, national security, medicine, animated films and robotics.

The Federal Government, mainly in the U.S. Department of Defense, employs many mathematicians. Some working for the Federal Government work for the National Institute of Standards and Technology or the National Aeronautics and Space Administration.

Mathematics Careers:

• Actuaries

• Mathematicians

• Operations Research Analysts

• Statisticians

Actuaries

People interested in an actuarial career typically need at least a Bachelor of Mathematics, Bachelor of Statistics, Bachelor of Business, or Bachelor of

Actuarial Science degree. Many actuarial students obtain an internship while in school.

Actuaries must pass multiple exams to become certified actuarial professionals; many employers expect actuaries to have passed at least one of these exams prior to graduating with their bachelor degree.

The Casualty Actuarial Society (CAS) and the Society of Actuaries (SOA) both offer two levels of certification: associate and fellowship

Certification through the SOA requires passing a series of five exams, plus seminars on professionalism.

Certification through the CAS requires passing a series of seven exams, plus seminars on professionalism.

Actuaries working in the property and casualty field become certified through the CAS, while actuaries working in the life insurance, health insurance, retirement benefits, investments, and finance receive certification through the SOA. Certification through either society takes four to six years. It generally takes actuaries two to three years to continue and earn fellowship status.

Essential Career Information

Median Pay$93,680

Entry-level education requirements Bachelor's degree

(source: Bureau of Labor and statistics)

Mathematicians

An entry-level position in a mathematician career requires at least a Bachelor of Mathematics or significant coursework in mathematics. Employers prefer candidates who double majored in mathematics and a related field such as computer science, engineering, or physical science.

In the private industry, mathematicians typically need a minimum of a Master of Applied Mathematics or Master of Theoretical Mathematics. Mathematicians don't need specific certifications or licenses.

Essential Career Information

Median Pay $101,360

Entry-level education requirements Master's degree

(source: Bureau of labor statistics)

Operations Research Analysts

An operations research analyst career begins with a minimum of a Bachelor of Operations Research degree, a Bachelor of Management Science degree, a Bachelor in Mathematical

Sciences or a bachelor's degree in a related field such as engineering, physics, mathematics, or computer science.

Most operations research analyst jobs beyond an entry-level job require a master's degree such as a Master's degree in Operations Research or a Master's degree in Management Science.

Operations research analysts don't need specific licenses or certification, however taking continuing education courses throughout their career helps them keep up with technology advances.

Essential Career Information

Median Pay$72,100

Entry-level education requirements Bachelor's degree

(source: Bureau of Labor Statistics)

Statisticians

A statistician career typically begins with a Master of Statistics, Master of Mathematics, or Master of Survey Methodology degree. Occasionally, a statistician may obtain an entry-level position with a bachelor degree, but a master's degree is increasingly the standard. Research and academic statistician jobs usually require a Ph.D. No specific certification or license is required for statisticians.

Essential Career Information

Median Pay$75,560

Life, Physical, and Social Sciences

The life, physical and social sciences sectors provide a wide variety of interesting careers. The sectors provide administrative, management, technician and research jobs.

Many of the life, physical and social sciences careers require at least a bachelor degree, however many of the careers require a graduate degree, specific training and experience. In the life sciences sector over 50 percent of medical and other life scientists have a doctoral degree.

Most scientists work in the private sector, about 27 percent of scientists work for federal, state and local government agencies.

Life sciences careers typically involve study living organisms. Physical science careers typically involve the study and application of the principles of chemistry and physics.

Professionals with social sciences careers examine human society and relationships of individuals. Social sciences careers may involve performing research or other professional or scientific work in one field or a combination of social sciences fields. The social sciences sector also includes a variety of administrative and management positions.

Life, Physical, and Social Sciences Careers:

- Agricultural and Food Science Technicians
- Agricultural and Food Scientists
- Anthropologists and Archeologists
- Atmospheric Scientists and Meteorologists
- Biochemists and Biophysicists
- Chemical Technicians
- Chemists and Materials Scientists
- Conservation Scientists and Foresters

- Economists
- Environmental Science and Protection Technicians
- Environmental Scientists and Specialists
- Epidemiologists
- Forensic Science Technicians
- Forest and Conservation Technicians
- Geographers
- Geological and Petroleum Technicians
- Geoscientists
- Historians
- Hydrologists
- Medical Scientists
- Microbiologists
- Natural Sciences Managers
- Nuclear Technicians
- Physicists and Astronomers
- Political Scientists
- Psychologists
- Sociologists
- Survey Researchers
- Urban and Regional Planners
- Zoologists and Wildlife Biologists

Agricultural and Food Science Technicians

Agricultural and food science technologists generally need an Associate in Animal Science degree or an Associate in Food Science degree or an associate's degree in a related field. Some schools offer an Associate in Agricultural Technology Food Science degree.

Many schools offer internships, cooperative education and other experiential programs for food technologists.

People who choose food science careers but have only a high school diploma usually undertake an extensive training program that can last a year or more.

Essential Career Information

Median Pay$34,070

Entry-level education requirements Associate's degree

Agricultural and Food Scientists

People need at least a bachelor's degree in agricultural science, biology, chemistry or physics to begin an agricultural science career or a food scientist career. Botany, chemistry and plant conservation degrees provide good preparation for soil and plant science work.

Organizations such as the American Registry of Professional Animal Scientists certify agricultural scientists and food scientists recognized for expertise in this field. While not required, the agriculture and food science industry recognize the value of certification. Some states do require licensing for soil scientists.

Essential Career Information

Median Pay$58,070

Entry-level education requirements Bachelor's degree

Anthropologists and Archeologists

Candidates need a master's degree to pursue an anthropology career or an archeology career. Leadership roles and jobs requiring more technical expertise may necessitate a doctoral degree; especially true when it comes to anthropology or archeology projects outside the country. Those who have a bachelor's degree may find lab or field work.

Many colleges and universities offer a Master in Cultural Anthropology degree, a Master in Physical Anthropology, a Ph.D. in Anthropology or a graduate forensic anthropology program.

Essential Career Information

Median Pay$57,420

Entry-level education requirements Master's degree

Personal Care and Service

The personal care and services sectors include a variety of careers and a large number of workers. Personal care and services careers attract people who enjoy being involved with other people throughout the work day.

Some of the personal care and services jobs require a state license. Some schools provide specialized education programs for people interested in personal care and services careers. The length of these education programs ranges from several weeks to two years.

Personal Care Careers:

• Animal Care & Service Workers

• Barbers, Hairdressers & Cosmetologists

• Childcare Workers

• Fitness Trainers & Instructors

• Funeral Directors

• Gaming Services Workers

• Home Health Aides & Personal Care Aides

• Manicurists & Pedicurists

• Massage Therapists

• Recreation Workers

• Skincare Specialists

• Travel Agents

Animal Care and Service Workers

People interested in an animal care worker career or an animal service worker career, frequently learn on-the-job, but many employers require candidates to have a high school diploma. Some community college and vocational programs serve people who want to train dogs or horses.

In some cases, a college degree helps; zoos typically seek animal care technicians with a bachelor's degree in biology, animal science or a similar field.

Animal care workers seeking to serve as pet groomers have the option of attending a state-licensed grooming school.

Animal care workers who choose to work at a marina may need a bachelor's degree in marine biology, animal science or a related field.

Essential Career Information

Median Pay$20,840

Entry-level education requirements None

Barbers, Hairdressers and Cosmetologists

Those who choose a barber career, a hairdresser career or a cosmetologist career need a high school diploma or equivalent and complete a state-licensed program in hairstyling, skin care or similar area. High schools and vocational schools offer barber, hairdresser and cosmetology courses, sometimes leading to an associate's degree. Those who work solely as shampooers need no formal education. All barbers, hairstylists and cosmetologists must pass a state licensing exam.

Essential Career Information

Median Pay$22,700

Entry-level education requirements Vocational training

Childcare Workers

Requirements for people seeking a childcare worker career vary among states, employers and the goals of the job. Some states require those who choose a childcare career to have a high school diploma, and many require daycare providers and family childcare providers to have a license.

Becoming a licensed center or daycare provider involves staff background checks, complete immunization records and a minimum training requirement.

While some states have no requirements for childcare workers, some employers require an associate's degree in early childhood education or a child development credential.

States often require daycare workers to have Child Development Associate certification through the Council for Professional Recognition. The certification requires coursework, experience and a high school diploma. Median Pay$19,510

Fitness Trainers and Instructors

Educational requirements for those who choose a fitness trainer career or fitness instructor career depend on the specialty involved. Many employers prefer to hire certified fitness trainers. Personal fitness trainer, group fitness instructor and specialized fitness instructor require different skills.

Some employers seek applicants with a bachelor's degree in physical education, physical fitness or exercise science.

People seeking a personal trainer career often need certification to work with clients or members of gyms or health clubs. Most fitness trainers or fitness instructors need CPR certification before getting their physical fitness certification. Basic certification requires no specific training or education; however, fitness trainers and fitness instructors can take exams, workshops and seminars.

Essential Career Information

Median Pay$31,720

Entry-level education requirements High school diploma or equivalent

Health care support

The thriving healthcare field offers some of the nation's best career opportunities. If you're seeking a personally and financially rewarding career, consider the healthcare industry. Well-paid healthcare professionals work with caring co-workers to improve peoples' lives.

Due to the increasing larger elderly population the demand for healthcare and medical professionals continues to increase. The healthcare and medical sectors encompass an array of rewarding careers. The health/medical industry continually seeks qualified professionals for a variety of healthcare careers and medical careers.

Many healthcare careers only require a two-year degree or a certificate. Many of the health careers and medical careers require people to complete a licensure program or course training. Many of the careers in health and medical technology require specific certifications.

Medical Careers:

• Cardiovascular Technologists and Technicians and Vascular Technologists

• Diagnostic Medical Sonographers

• EMTs and Paramedics

• Home Health Aides and Personal Care Aides

• Licensed Practical Nurses (LPNs) and Licensed Vocational Nurses (LVNs)

• Medical and Clinical Laboratory Technologists and Technicians

• Medical and Health Services Managers

• Medical Appliance Technicians

• Medical Assistants

• Medical Equipment Repairers

• Medical Records and Health Information Technicians

• Medical Scientists

• Medical Transcriptionists

• Nursing Aides, Orderlies, and Attendants

• Physician Assistants

• Physicians and Surgeons

- Psychiatric Technicians and Psychiatric Aides

- Radiation Therapists

- Radiologic Technologists

- Registered Nurses

Cardiovascular Technologists and Technicians and Vascular Technologists

People interested in a cardiovascular technologist, cardiovascular technician or vascular technician career generally need an Associate of Radiologic Technology degree or an Associate of Nursing degree. However, some cardiovascular technologists have a Bachelor of Radiologic Technology degree.

In most programs, associates or bachelors, students work with an experienced technologists or technician in a lab setting for course credit. Some schools provide an Associate in Cardiovascular Sonography degree.

Some community colleges offer one-year certifications for individuals who have already received training in a medical field.

A cardiovascular technician working as an EKG technician usually receives 4-6 weeks of on-the-job training from their employer.

Cardiovascular technologists, cardiovascular technicians and vascular technicians do not require certification, but it's highly recommended, as most employers prefer certification. Many insurance providers only pay for work conducted by a certified cardiovascular technologist, a certified cardiovascular technician, or a certified vascular technician.

A variety of certifications for cardiovascular technologists, cardiovascular technicians, or vascular technicians exist, depending on their clinical focus, and they may become certified in multiple areas. In most cases, cardiovascular technologists, cardiovascular technicians, or vascular technicians must take continuing education courses to maintain their certification.

Essential Career Information

Median Pay$52,070

Entry-level education requirements Associate's degree

Diagnostic Medical Sonographers

Individuals seeking a diagnostic medical sonographer career typically need an Associate of Sonography or a postsecondary certificate from an accredited institute or hospital program. Colleges offer an Associate in Sonography degree and a Bachelor in Sonography degree. Some colleges offer an Associate in Cardiovascular Sonography degree program or an Associate in Diagnostic Medical Sonography degree program.

Individuals already involved in the healthcare field can obtain a one-year certificate. Some sonographers obtain a degree in radiologic technology or nursing, then receiving on–the-job training.

Many employers prefer or even require a professional certification. Certification involves graduating from an accredited program and passing an exam related to the specialty the diagnostic medial sonographer is most interested in. Diagnostic medical sonographers must also take continuing education courses to keep their certification up-to-date.

Some states also require licensure for diagnostic medical sonographers. Requirements for licensure vary by state.

Essential Career Information

Median Pay$65,860

Entry-level education requirements

• Associate's degree

EMTs and Paramedics

Individuals interested in an EMT career or a paramedic career need to have a high school diploma, or equivalent, cardiopulmonary resuscitation (CPR) certification, and a state license.

People interested in an EMT career or a paramedic career can obtain formal training from technical institutes, community colleges, and other facilities specializing in emergency care training.

EMT-Basics have the least amount of training, while paramedics have the most amount of training. Paramedics may obtain their training through a community college, earning an associate's degree.

EMTs and paramedics must take a course and become certified to drive an ambulance.

EMTs and paramedics may be certified by the National Registry of Emergency Medical Technicians (NREMT) on four different levels: EMT-Basic, EMT-Intermediate 1985, EMT-Intermediate 1999, and Paramedic. Some states have their own certification and may use different titles for the same positions.

EMTs and paramedics must obtain a state license, the requirements vary by state.

Essential Career Information

Median Pay$31,020

Entry-level education requirements

• Post-secondary non-degree award

Home Health Aides and Personal Care Aides

Most home health care aides and personal care aides have a high school diploma, although no specific education requirements exist for this position. Home health aides and personal care aides typically receive on-the-job training. Some employers may require a competency evaluation prior to hire.

Some states have no training requirement for home health aides and personal care aides, but other states require a formal training from a community college, vocational school, elder care program, or home health care agency. Some states also require a background check for all home health aides and personal care aides.

Home health care aides working for an employer receiving reimbursements from Medicare or Medicaid must obtain training and pass a competency evaluation or earn a state certification.

Home health aides and personal care aides may receive certification from the National Association for Home Care and Hospice (NAHC). Certification is not required, but many employers prefer to hire certified workers.

Essential Career Information

Median Pay$19,910

Entry-level education requirements: Less than high school

Transportation Careers

More than eight million Americans have transportation jobs, including over three million truck drivers who transport raw materials and products throughout the nation. A growing population increases the demand for products which creates growth in the transportation industry.

Some transportation careers require postsecondary education, whereas other transportation careers require training obtained through a trade school or on-the-job training. Transportation careers such as pilot, air traffic controller and postal worker require extensive, specialized training.

The transportation industry also includes clerical and management jobs. Typically, a transportation manager oversees all transportation services for a company.

Transportation Careers:
• Automotive Service Technicians and Mechanics

• Bus Drivers

• Cargo and Freight Agents

• Delivery Truck Drivers and Driver/Sales Workers

• Diesel Service Technicians and Mechanics

• Heavy and Tractor-Trailer Truck Drivers

• Heavy Vehicle and Mobile Equipment Service Technicians

• Material Moving Machine Operators

Automotive Service Technicians and Mechanics

A vocational or postsecondary training program in automotive service technology is the new standard for automotive technician and automotive mechanic entry-level jobs. Automotive service technology programs typically last six months to one year, although some schools offer a two-year Associate in Automotive Service Technology degree program. Automotive manufacturers and dealers sponsor many of the associate's degree programs.

An automotive service technician career typically begins with on-the-job training, working under the instruction of an experienced technician for two to five years before being considered a fully qualified service technician. Automotive service technicians generally work another one to two years before becoming familiar with all types of repairs.

Automotive service technicians working with refrigerant are required by the U.S. Environmental Protection Agency to obtain a license in proper refrigerant handling.

Most employers require automotive service technicians to become certified from the National Institute of Automotive Service Excellence. Automotive service technicians can become certified in any of the following: automatic transmission/transaxle, brakes, electrical/electronic systems, engine performance, engine repair, heating and air conditioning, manual drive train and axles, or suspension and steering. A Master Automotive Technician has certification in all eight areas.

The Certified Professional Manufacturers' Representative (CPMR) certification or the Certified Sales Professional (CSP) demonstrates industry credibility.

Essential Career Information

Median Pay$36,610

Entry-level education requirements High school diploma or equivalent

Bus Drivers

People interested in a bus driver career, typically need a commercial driver's license (CDL) and training and they must meet hearing and vision test standards. Training consists of one to three months practicing bus maneuvers and light traffic driving that leads to practice runs on specific routes. Experienced bus drivers accompany the new trainees and provide performance evaluations.

Bus drivers need to pass a written test and a driving test to obtain a commercial driver's license (CDL). Bus drivers may also need special endorsements to drive a school or passenger bus. People need to pass knowledge and driving tests to obtain a school (S) endorsement or a passenger (P) endorsement. Bus drivers also must pass random drug and alcohol tests during their bus driver career.

Essential Career Information

Median Pay$36,600

Entry-level education requirements High school diploma or equivalent

Cargo and Freight Agents

Typically, people interested in a freight career need a high school diploma or a GED and on-the-job training. As training progresses, cargo agents take on more complex jobs such as notifying customers of shipment times and deliveries as well as monitoring shipments in route.

Cargo and freight agents use specific shipment software programs and computer databases which require a short time of computer training.

Essential Career Information

Median Pay$39,720

Employment growth forecast, 2010-202029 percent

Entry-level education requirements High school diploma or equivalent

Delivery Truck Drivers and Driver/Sales Workers

People interested in a delivery truck driver career or a driver/sales worker career need a high school diploma or equivalent and a state issued driver's license and undergo less than one month of training on the job. The training typically includes working with an experienced driver who rides along with a new worker to make sure that he/she can operate and handle a truck in difficult road conditions. In addition, drivers may also take classes from their employer to learn policies and procedures.

Median Pay$22,670

Engineering and Architecture

Most architects get their training through a five-year bachelor of architecture degree program; some earn a master's such as a Master of Architecture which can take one to five years depending on previous education and experience.

All states require architects to obtain a license, which can include a professional degree in architecture, practical training and internship. An architect must also pass the Architect Registration Examination. Most states require continuing education to maintain licensure.

Engineering, a broad field, includes an array of rewarding specialties; most engineers specialize in an area. Qualified engineers are in demand in a variety of fields.

Typically, engineers need math and science knowledge. People seeking an engineering career typically need a bachelor degree in engineering or in a relevant field. Some engineering jobs, especially in management, require a master's degree. An engineering degree in a specialty area may qualify engineers for an engineering career in another applicable area.

Many engineers have rewarding careers working on cutting edge technology. Many engineering jobs involve computers. Due to the engineering sector relying on continual innovation, the best engineers enjoy a changing work environment. Engineers often work as a team to come up with new innovations.

A study performed by the U.S. Department of Labor shows professional engineers tend to stay employed with the same company for significantly longer periods of time than workers in other professions.

Engineering Careers:

• Aerospace Engineering and Operations Technicians

• Aerospace Engineers

• Agricultural Engineers

• Biomedical Engineers

• Cartographers and Photogrammetrists

- Chemical Engineers

- Civil Engineering Technicians

- Civil Engineers

- Electrical and Electronic Engineering Technicians

- Electrical and Electronics Engineers

- Electro-Mechanical Technicians

- Engineering Managers

- Environmental Engineers

- Health and Safety Engineers

- Industrial Engineering Technicians

- Marine Engineers and Naval Architects

- Materials Engineers

- Mechanical Engineering Technicians

- Mechanical Engineers

- Mining and Geological Engineers

- Nuclear Engineers

- Petroleum Engineers

- Sales Engineers

- Surveying and Mapping Technicians

- Surveyors

Aerospace Engineering and Operations Technicians

Candidates for avionics technicians' jobs should be detail-oriented and have good communication, critical-thinking, math, technical and interpersonal skills.

Certification is not required to work as an aerospace technician, but skills-based programs can help you earn certification through the Federal Aviation Commission, which can increase your hiring potential.

Certificate and diploma programs offered by vocational-technical schools provide training for work as an aerospace technician, but employers increasingly seek candidates with an associate in aerospace engineering technology degree. Aerospace technicians seeking to work on defense contracts must qualify for a security clearance, which sometimes requires U.S. citizenship.

Essential Career Information

Median Pay$61,460

Entry-level education requirements Associate's degree

Aerospace Engineers

An entry-level aerospace engineer may need a bachelor's degree in aerospace engineering or a related field.

Candidates for an aerospace engineer career need analytical and critical thinking skills and the ability to handle complex problem-solving. Many aeronautical engineers work on defense projects for the U.S. government, which requires a security clearance.

Some schools partner with companies to give prospective aerospace engineers practical experience while earning their degree. Some universities also offer five-year programs for candidates to earn both a bachelor's and a master's degree in aeronautical engineering. Advanced education may qualify an aerospace engineer to teach or work in product research and development.

Aerospace engineers who gain experience and want to take on more responsibility must earn a license as a professional engineer, which generally requires a degree from an accredited engineering program and passing scores on the Fundamentals of Engineering and the Professional Engineering exams.

Aeronautical engineers can take the Fundamentals of Engineering exam after earning a bachelor's degree, at which point they serve as engineers-in-training or engineer interns to acquire enough experience to take the Principles and Practice of Engineering exam.

Aerospace engineers in several states must take continuing education courses to maintain their licenses.

Essential Career Information

Median Pay$ 102,420

Entry-level education requirements Bachelor's degree

Maintenance and Repair Careers

Since most items mechanical in nature or which use electricity must be installed, maintenance or repaired, skilled installation, maintenance and repair technicians have plenty of work opportunities.

Maintenance technicians play an important role in the repair and upkeep of equipment, machines and buildings. Their work environment depends on their specialization and employer. Maintenance technicians are also known as machinery maintenance workers, industrial machinery mechanics and electro-mechanical technicians.

There's an array of installation, maintenance and repair careers to choose from. These careers are available in a variety of settings. Some installation, maintenance and repair careers require on-the-job training, whereas some of these careers require the completion of a formal training program.

Maintenance and Repair Careers:

• Aircraft and Avionics Equipment Mechanics and Technicians

• Automotive Body and Glass Repairers

• Automotive Service Technicians and Mechanics

• Computer, ATM, and Office Machine Repairers

• Diesel Service Technicians and Mechanics

• Electrical and Electronic Installers and Repairers

• General Maintenance and Repair Workers

• Heating, Air Conditioning and Refrigeration Mechanics and Installers

• Heavy Vehicle and Mobile Equipment Service Technicians

• Home Appliance Repairers

- Industrial Machinery Mechanics and Machinery Maintenance Workers
- Line Installers and Repairers
- Medical Appliance Technicians
- Medical Equipment Repairers
- Millwrights
- Small Engine Mechanics
- Telecommunications Equipment Installers and Repairers

Automotive Body and Glass Repairers

Automotive body and glass repairers restore, refinish, and replace vehicle bodies and frames, windshields, and window glass.

Essential requirement

Education requirement High school diploma or equivalent

Median pay $40,580

Automotive service technicians and mechanics

Automotive service technicians and mechanics, often called service technicians or service techs, inspect, maintain, and repair cars and light trucks.

Essential requirement

Education requirement Postsecondary nondegree award

Median pay $39,550

Management Careers

Skilled managers are in demand in an array of industries. Managers with the appropriate experience and credentials are some of the world's highest paid professionals.

The three basic management levels include top-level manager, middle manager and lower manager. People seeking a management careers need skills such as leadership, communication, motivational and interpersonal.

The major industries providing management careers include healthcare facilities, wholesalers, banks, business service companies, government agencies, insurance companies, retail businesses and schools.

Education requirements for management jobs vary by the company or organization. Some employers require a bachelor degree or an associate degree or some post-secondary education. Some management jobs require a Master in Business Administration (MBA) degree or a master degree in another field.

Management Careers:
• Administrative Services Managers
• Advertising, Promotions, and Marketing Managers
• Architectural and Engineering Managers
• Compensation and Benefits Managers
• Computer and Information Systems Managers
• Engineering Managers
• Farmers, Ranchers and Other Agricultural Managers
• Financial Managers
• Food Service Managers
• Human Resources Managers
• Industrial Production Managers
• Legislators
• Lodging Managers
• Management Analysts
• Medical and Health Services Managers
• Natural Sciences Managers
• Post-secondary Education Administrators
• Preschool and Childcare Center Directors

- Property, Real Estate, and Community Association Managers
- Public Relations Managers and Specialists
- Sales Managers
- Social and Community Service Managers
- Top Executives

Administrative Services Managers

Administrative services managers plan, direct, and coordinate supportive services of an organization. Their specific responsibilities vary, but administrative service managers typically maintain facilities and supervise activities that include recordkeeping, mail distribution, and office upkeep.

Essential career information

Education requirement Bachelor's degree

Median pay $94,020

Advertising, Promotions, and Marketing Managers

Advertising, promotions, and marketing managers plan programs to generate interest in products or services. They work with art directors, sales agents, and financial staff members.

Essential career information

Education requirement Bachelor's degree

Median pay $129,380

Architectural and Engineering Managers

Architectural and engineering managers plan, direct, and coordinate activities in architectural and engineering companies.

Essential career information

Education requirement Bachelor's degree

Median pay $137,720

Art and Media

The dynamic world of art and design provides an array of career opportunities from designing floral arrangements to creating movie sets. The range of art and design careers provides opportunities for just about every creative person. Art and design careers such as graphic designer and interior designer combine creativity with practical skills, whereas a fashion designer career relies more on creativity.

Just about every sector needs people with art and design degrees for rewarding niche roles. People with art and design careers use their creative skills to communicate their client's message. The art and design sector can be quite competitive, with technical skills increasingly important for many art and design jobs.

Freelance artists who sell their own artwork benefit from more artistic freedom, flexible scheduling and the ability to select their projects. They must manage their finances, marketing and public relations.

Art Careers:

• Art Directors

• Craft and Fine Artists

• Fashion Designers

• Floral Designers

• Graphic Designers

• Industrial Designers

• Interior Designers

• Jewelers and Precious Stone and Metal Workers

• Multimedia Artists and Animators

• Set and Exhibit Designers

Art Directors

An art director career typically requires a Bachelor of Arts or Bachelor of Fine Arts and three to five years of previous work experience in a related position, such as graphic designer, illustrator, copyeditor, or photographer.

Some colleges and universities offer a Bachelor of Design, a Bachelor of Visual Communications, a Bachelor in Multimedia Design and Development, a Bachelor in Design Management, a Bachelor in Graphic Design, or a Bachelor in Digital Media degree program.

Some art directors hoping to advance in their career continue their education with a Master of Fine Arts (MFA) or Master of Business Administration (MBA) degree.

Art directors don't need a specific license or certification.

Media Careers:

• Announcers

• Art Directors

• Broadcast and Sound Engineering Technicians

• Editors

• Film and Video Editors and Camera Operators

• Graphic Designers

• Interpreters and Translators

• Photographers

• Reporters, Correspondents, and Broadcast News Analysts

• Technical Writers

• Writers and Authors

The media/news/communications industry has an array of rewarding careers for dedicated professionals with good communications skills. The increasingly popular online media provides an array of job opportunities.

Technology provides more opportunities for the media/news/ communications industry to offer audio and visual messages to the public.

People seeking a media, news or communications career benefit from gaining experience through an internship or through working for a college newspaper. Some of the careers in the media/news/communications industry require a bachelor degree.

Business and Finance Careers

Business careers are available in just about every industry. People with business skills are in demand in large corporations, small companies, non-profits and government agencies. Business careers provide viable ways to build long, rewarding careers.

Due to the vast nature of the business world, there are no required set of skills, each career has its unique requirements, some business careers require an aptitude for math, whereas other business careers require excellent communications and interpersonal skills.

Business and Finance careers

- Actuaries

- Accountants and Auditors

- Appraisers and Assessors of Real Estate

- Budget Analysts

- Claims Adjusters, Appraisers, Examiners, and Investigators

- Cost Estimators

- Financial Analysts

- Financial Clerks

- Human Resources Specialists

- Insurance Underwriters

- Loan Officers

- Logisticians

- Management Analysts

- Market Research Analysts

- Meeting, Convention and Events Planners

- Operations Research Analysts

- Personal Financial Advisors
- Purchasing Managers, Buyers and Purchasing Agents
- Statisticians

Accountants and Auditors

Accountants and auditors prepare and examine financial records. They ensure that financial records are accurate and that taxes are paid properly and on time. Accountants and auditors assess financial operations and work to help ensure that organizations run efficiently.

Essential career information

Education requirement Bachelor's degree

Median pay $69,350

Appraisers and Assessors of Real Estate

Appraisers and assessors of real estate provide a value estimate on land and buildings usually before they are sold, mortgaged, taxed, insured, or developed.

Essential career information

Education requirement: Bachelor's degree

2017 median pay $54,010

Budget analysts

Budget analysts help public and private institutions organize their finances. They prepare budget reports and monitor institutional spending.

Essential career information

Education requirement: Bachelor's degree

2017 median pay $75,240

Administrative work

Administrative support employees work in practically every industry. Duties vary by the specific office assistant job and company, however duties for often assistants typically involve clerical tasks and back-office duties. Many administrative assistant jobs provide opportunities for increases in pay and career advancement.

Administrative Support and Clerical Careers:

• Administrative Services Managers

• Bill and Account Collectors

• Bookkeepers and Accounting and Auditing Clerks

• Cargo and Freight Agents

• Couriers and Messengers

• Customer Service Representatives

• Desktop Publishers

• Financial Clerks

• General Office Clerks

• Information Clerks

• Medical Records and Health Information Technicians

• Paralegals and Legal Assistants

• Secretaries and Administrative Assistants

Community and Social Service

Community and social service occupations include social workers, counselors, and religious workers. Employment of community and social service occupations is projected to grow 14 percent from 2016 to 2026, faster than the average for all occupations, adding about 371,900 jobs. Most projected new jobs in this occupational group are in counselor and social worker occupations, as their services will continue to be needed in areas such as drug abuse counseling and rehabilitation counseling, and for school and career counseling.

The median annual wage for community and social service occupations was $43,840 in May 2017, which was higher than the median annual wage for all occupations of $37,690.

Social and Human Service Assistants

Social and human service assistants provide client services, including support for families, in a wide variety of fields, such as psychology, rehabilitation, and social work. They assist other workers, such as social workers, and they help clients find benefits or community services.

Essential career information:

Entry level education: High school diploma or equivalent

2017 median pay $33,120

(source: bureau of labor statistics)

Rehabilitation Counselors

Rehabilitation counselors help people with physical, mental, developmental, or emotional disabilities live independently. They work with clients to overcome or manage the personal, social, or psychological effects of disabilities on employment or independent living.

Essential career information

Entry requirement: Master's degree

2017 median pay $34,860

(source: Bureau of labor statistics)

Substance abuse and behavioral disorder counselors

Substance abuse, behavioral disorder, and mental health counselors advise people who suffer from alcoholism, drug addiction, eating disorders, mental health issues, or other mental or behavioral problems. They provide treatment and support to help clients recover from addiction or modify problem behaviors. Median pay $43,300

Health educators

Health educators teach people about behaviors that promote wellness. They develop and implement strategies to improve the health of individuals and communities. Community health workers collect data and discuss health concerns with members of specific populations or communities.

Median pay $45,360

Social Workers

Social workers help people solve and cope with problems in their everyday lives. Clinical social workers also diagnose and treat mental, behavioral, and emotional issues.

Median pay $47,980

Mental health counselors and marriage and family therapists

Marriage and family therapists help people manage and overcome problems with family and other relationships.

Essential information

Entry requirement Master's degree

Median pay $48,790

(source: Bureau of labor statistics)

Probation officers and correctional treatment specialists

Probation officers and correctional treatment specialists provide social services to assist in rehabilitation of law offenders in custody or on probation or parole.

Essential career information

Entry requirement Bachelor's degree

Median pay $51,410

School and Career Counselors

School counselors help students develop the academic and social skills needed to succeed in school. Career counselors help people choose careers and follow a path to employment.

Entry requirement to the profession is master's degree and the median pay is $55,410

Education Careers

The education sector provides rewarding education careers such as elementary school teacher and special education teacher. The education field offers careers besides teaching careers such as instructional coordinator, archivist and librarian. A lot of the education careers require postsecondary education and strong interpersonal skills.

Every state requires school teachers to have certification. State education boards provide certification to teachers for specific grade levels or specific subjects. Teachers need to have a bachelor's degree and complete a training program, including student teaching. Sometimes specialty teachers need to have a master's degree.

Education Careers:

• Adult Literacy & GED Teachers

• Archivists

• Career Teachers & Technical Education Teachers

• Curators, Museum Technicians & Conservators

• Health Educators

• High School Teachers

• Instructional Coordinators

• Kindergarten & Elementary School Teachers

- Librarians

- Library Technicians & Assistants

- Middle School Teachers

- Post-Secondary Education Administrators

- Postsecondary Teachers

- Preschool & Childcare Center Directors

- Preschool Teachers

- School & Career Counselors

- Self-Enrichment Teachers

- Special Education Teachers

- Teacher Assistants

Legal Occupations

Employment of legal occupations is projected to grow 9 percent from 2016 to 2026, about as fast as the average for all occupations, which will result in about 116,200 new jobs. As law firms try to increase the efficiency of legal services and reduce their costs, there is expected to be strong demand to hire many more paralegals and legal assistants. Additionally, the demand for lawyers is expected to continue as individuals, businesses, and governments require legal services in many areas.

The median annual wage for legal occupations was $80,080 in May 2017, which was higher than the median annual wage for all occupations of $37,690.

Arbitrators, Mediators, and Conciliators

Arbitrators, mediators, and conciliators facilitate negotiation and dialogue between disputing parties to help resolve conflicts outside of the court system.

Entry requirement: Bachelor's degree

2017 Median pay $60,670

Court reporters

Court reporters create word-for-word transcriptions at trials, depositions, and other legal proceedings. Some court reporters provide captioning for television and real-time translation for deaf or hard-of-hearing people at public events, in business meetings, or in classrooms.

Entry requirement: Postsecondary nanodegree award

2017 median pay $55,120

Judges, mediators, and hearing officers

Judges and hearing officers apply the law by overseeing the legal process in courts. They also conduct pretrial hearings, resolve administrative disputes, facilitate negotiations between opposing parties, and issue legal decisions.

Entry requirement: Doctoral or professional degree

2017 median pay $115,520

Lawyers

Lawyers advise and represent individuals, businesses, and government agencies on legal issues and disputes.

Entry requirement: Doctoral or professional degree

2017 median pay $119,250

Paralegals and legal assistants

Paralegals and legal assistants perform a variety of tasks to support lawyers, including maintaining and organizing files, conducting legal research, and drafting documents.

Entry requirement Associate's degree

2017 median pay $50,410

Protective Service

Employment of protective service occupations is projected to grow 5 percent from 2016 to 2026, about as fast as the average for all occupations, which will result in about 158,200 new jobs.

Protective service occupations had a median annual wage of $39,550 in May 2017, which was slightly higher than the median annual wage for all occupations of $37,690.

Correctional officers and Bailiffs

Correctional officers are responsible for overseeing individuals who have been arrested and are awaiting trial or who have been sentenced to serve time in jail or prison. Bailiffs are law enforcement officers who maintain safety and order in courtrooms.

Entry requirements: High school diploma or equivalent

2017 median pay $43,510

Fire inspectors and investigators

Fire inspectors examine buildings in order to detect fire hazards and ensure that federal, state, and local fire codes are met. Fire investigators, another type of worker in this field, determine the origin and cause of fires and explosions. Forest fire inspectors and prevention specialists assess outdoor fire hazards in public and residential areas.

2017 median pay $56,670

Firefighters

Firefighters control and put out fires and respond to emergencies where life, property, or the environment is at risk.

Education requirement Postsecondary nondegree award

2017 median pay $49,080

Police and Detectives

Police officers protect lives and property. Detectives and criminal investigators, who are sometimes called agents or special agents, gather facts and collect evidence of possible crimes.

2017 median pay $62,960

Private Detectives and Investigators

Private detectives and investigators search for information about legal, financial, and personal matters. They offer many services, such as verifying people's backgrounds and statements, finding missing persons, and investigating computer crimes.

Education requirement: High school diploma or equivalent

2017 median pay $50,700

Security Guards and Gaming Surveillance Officers

Security guards and gaming surveillance officers patrol and protect property against theft, vandalism, and other illegal activity.

Education requirement: High school diploma or equivalent

2017 median pay $26,960

Coping with Culture Shock in the United States will make your life easier

Understanding what culture shock is and how it comes about will help you identify it more easily and make your international move a little easier. The online Oxford Dictionary defines culture shock as disorientation experienced when suddenly subjected to an unfamiliar culture or way of life. This is a good summary. However, when you move to a new country, everything is unfamiliar; weather, landscape, language, food, dress, social roles, values, customs, and communication - basically, everything you're used to is no longer in place.

According to the website Global perspectives, "Culture shock is a common phenomenon and, though it may take months to develop, it often affects travelers and people living far from home in unexpected ways. Culture shock is more than simply being unfamiliar with social norms or experiencing new foods and it tends to impact people even after they've become familiar with and comfortable in new cultures. Culture shock generally moves through four different phases: honeymoon, frustration, adjustment and acceptance. While individuals experience these stages differently and the impact and order of each stage varies widely, they do provide a guideline of how we adapt and cope with new cultures".

1. The Honeymoon Stage

The first stage of culture shock is often overwhelmingly positive during which travelers become infatuated with the language, people and food in their new surroundings. At this stage, the trip or move seems like the greatest decision ever made, an exciting adventure to stay on forever. This happened to me when I first Landed in Detroit Michigan and later in a smaller airport in Vermont. The whole experience was exciting, and my hotel room was something out of this world, I loved each moment. Remember that on short trips, the honeymoon phase may take over the entire experience as the later effects of culture shock don't have time to set in. However, on longer trips, the honeymoon stage will usually phase out eventually.

2. The Frustration Stage

"Frustration may be the most difficult stage of culture shock and is probably familiar to anyone who has lived abroad or who travels frequently. At this stage, the fatigue of not understanding gestures, signs and the language sets in and miscommunications may be happening frequently". During the frustration stage, I had to learn more about transportation. Taking the bus was the worst experience especially during the winter and snow. It was a frustrating experience because I did not know how to drive. Don't be like me! Come to America equipped with driving skills. Public transportation in the United States is not dependable therefore be ready to drive your own personal car. "Bouts of depression or homesickness and feelings of longing to go home where things are familiar and comfortable are all common during the frustration stage ". Therefore, do not give up, focus on why you immigrated to the United States because eventually things will get better. People have done it and you can survive culture shock too. My general advice is do not compare America to your home country, instead learn how to adapt because America is not the issue believe me, the issue is that you must accept changes and adapt to your new country.

3. The Adjustment Stage

Frustrations are often subdued as you begin to feel more familiar and comfortable with the cultures, people, food and languages of new environments. Traveling becomes easier, friends and communities of support are established, and details of local languages may become more recognizable during the adjustment stage

https://medium.com/global-perspectives/the-4-stages-of-culture-shock-a79957726164

ETIQUETTE AND BEHAVIOR

In America I have learnt to maintain eye contact a sign of genuine and honest conversation. Avoid crossing arms which can be a sign of loss of interest in the conversation. A smile will go a long way to make others feel good. Every culture has its unspoken rules that govern how people interact with and treat one another. I hope you enjoyed this book; the information will cut your learning curve in the United States. I wish you success in your career ambitions.

49207611R00076

Made in the USA
Columbia, SC
17 January 2019